The Five Foundations of SMSFs

View Legal

Matthew Burgess

National Library of Australia Cataloguing-in-Publication entry

Creator: Burgess, Matthew, author.
Title: The Five Foundations of SMSFs / Matthew Burgess;
book designed by Dedicated Book Services.

ISBN: 978-1-925181-13-5 (paperback)
ISBN: 978-1-925181-14-2 (ebook: Kindle)
ISBN: 978-1-925181-19-7 (ebook: epub)

Subjects: Burgess, Matthew.
View Legal (Firm)
Legal services—Australia.
Superannuation—Australia
Finance, Personal—Australia.
Assets (Accounting)—Australia.
Tax planning—Australia.
Estate planning—Australia.

Other Creators/Contributors:
Dedicated Book Services, book designer.

Published by D & M Fancy Pastry in 2017
Book Design by Dedicated Book Services

Contents

About the Author

Matthew Burgess, together with Patrick Ellwood, Naomi Arnold and Tara Lucke are co-founders, of View Legal.

Having previously founded Australia's first virtual law firm as a wholly owned subsidiary of one of the country's leading independent law firms, View Legal is result focused and passionate about delivering new solutions in a way that aligns with their 'SPS'—Service and Price Satisfaction—guarantee.

As an author, Matthew is a recognised expert, who constantly creates innovative strategies for the growth, management and protection of wealth.

Published legal books include:

1. The Nine Steps to a Complete Estate Plan;
2. The Seven Foundations of Business Succession;
3. The Nine Foundations of Asset Protection;
4. The Seven Key Aspects of Testamentary Trusts;
5. The Six Foundations of the Taxation of Trusts;
6. 40 Forms of Trusts;
7. Estate Planning War Stories;
8. The Eight Key Aspects of SMSFs;
9. Five Essential Estate Planning Articles; and
10. Six Essential Structuring Articles.

Introduction

In recent years, the need for effective structuring of retirement savings has been brought into sharp focus for private investors and business owners alike.

The combination of fundamental changes to the taxation regime, the vast amounts of wealth accumulated within superannuation funds, for many the perceived lack of value delivered by industry funds and the increasing tendency for both business and personal relationships to be relatively short term (as opposed to lifelong) have meant that traditional approaches to superannuation have been revolutionised.

In this context, the use of SMSFs has become ubiquitous.

The range of fundamental issues that need to be considered in relation to establishing and successfully maintaining an SMSF is vast.

This book analyses the key aspects of SMSFs, in the following order:

- a glossary of abbreviations;
- b explanation of the structure of trusts generally, with particular reference to SMSFs;
- c overview of the fundamental aspects of SMSFs, using an example 'product disclosure statement' as the basis;
- d analysis of the main SMSF investment structures, including use of borrowing;
- e SMSFs, estate planning and asset protection;
- f death benefit nominations; and
- g key cases.

Glossary of abbreviations

ABN—Australian Business Number
ASIC—Australian Securities and Investments Commission
ATO—Australian Taxation Office
ARP—auto reversionary pension
Bankruptcy Act—Bankruptcy Act 1966 (Cth)
BDBN—binding death benefit nomination
CGT—capital gains tax
Corporations Act—The Corporations Act 2001 (Cth)
Disability Services Act—Disability Services Act 1986 (Cth)
GST—Goods and Services Tax
IHA—in-house asset
LPR—legal personal representative
PAYG—Pay As You Go
PDS—Product disclosure statement
SCT—Superannuation Complaints Tribunal
SG Act—*Superannuation Guarantee* (Administration) *Act 1992* (Cth)
SIS Act—*Superannuation Industry* (Supervision) *Act 1993* (Cth)
SIS Regulations—the regulations made under the SIS Act
SMSF—self managed superannuation fund
SPT—Superannuation Proceeds Trust
Tax Act—*Income Tax Assessment Act 1936* (Cth) and the *Income Tax Assessment Act 1997* (Cth) (together with regulations and public rulings issued under those Acts)
TFM—testator's family maintenance
TFN—Tax File Number
TRIS—Transition to Retirement Income Stream

Chapter 1

OVERVIEW OF THE FUNDAMENTAL ASPECTS OF SMSFS

Explanation of SMSFs

Arguably the best introduction to SMSFs is the PDS document that is required by legislation to be provided to any person considering the establishment, or becoming a member, of an SMSF.

Following the structure overview below, the balance of this chapter is largely based on a 'standard' PDS.

Many of the concepts mentioned in this chapter are explored in more detail elsewhere in the book.

As with most areas of the law, superannuation rules, particularly for SMSFs, change regularly due to government and ATO driven legislation amendments and the impact of court decisions. Specialist and specific advice should always be obtained at the time of addressing any of the issues covered in this book.

Structure overview

A trust is, in effect, simply a legal relationship where there is:

a a legal owner of property (the 'trustee');
b who holds the property ('trust property');
c for the benefit of others (the 'beneficiaries'); and
d pursuant to certain terms or rules ('trust deed').

In the context of an SMSF, the key point of slight differentiation is that the 'beneficiaries' are referred to as 'members'.

Diagrammatically, the structure of an SMSF is represented below:

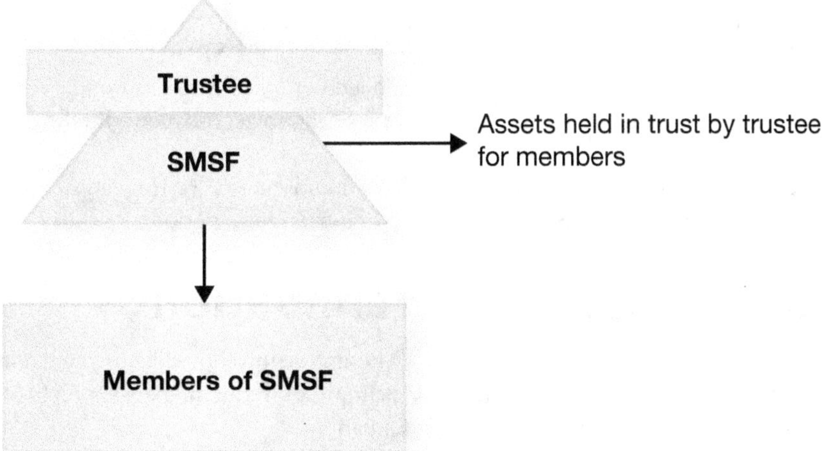

Trustee

The trustee is the legal owner of the property. The trustee will therefore have the ultimate control over the assets of the SMSF.

The trustee can be a company or one or more individuals, subject to rules set out under the SIS Act, as explained later in this book. Where the trustee is a company, the directors of the company will have the day-to-day control of the SMSF.

As the shareholders of the company appoint the directors, the shareholders will have the ultimate control over the SMSF, again however subject to the SIS Act rules.

Although the trustee is responsible for the day-to-day running of the SMSF, some deeds have a 'principal' (also commonly known as an appointor, guardian or nominator) who retains ultimate control over the SMSF. The principal has the ability to appoint and remove the trustee at any time, and its consent may be required to make any amendments to the trust deed.

If the trust deed does not name a principal, the existing trustee will usually have the power to appoint a new trustee.

Members

The SMSF structure enables income that is earned by the SMSF to be distributed to the members in accordance with their member balance, once a condition of release set out under the SIS Act is satisfied.

Trust deed

The trust deed of an SMSF sets out how the SMSF must be run, what the trustees can do in running the fund and who the members are.

The trust deed must comply with the provisions of the SIS Act.

It is necessary to review an SMSF trust deed periodically to ensure that it allows the trustees to operate the fund in effective way and in accordance with the current legislation.

Unlike most other forms of trusts, SMSFs do not have a 'vesting day' (or ending day). Generally non SMSF trusts can last for a maximum period of 80 years.

Investing via superannuation

A threshold issue in relation to SMSFs is whether wealth should be invested outside of the superannuation environment, for example, by reducing personal debt as opposed to making contributions to superannuation.

This decision will be affected by any array of variables, including:

a the member's current income and marginal tax rate;
b the member's existing assets and liabilities and the interest rates on borrowings;
c the risk profile of the member and what the intended investments inside and outside superannuation are likely to be (and therefore the potential investment returns of each investment);
d the age of the member, the time frame until they are able to access their superannuation (i.e. their preservation age) and whether they would be looking to retire earlier than their preservation age;
e whether the member has any dependants; and
f the security of the member's employment.

Factors in favour of superannuation investments

A summary of the factors that would support investment via superannuation include where the member:

a is nearing preservation age and intends to retire meaning that there is only a short period of time between when they make the contributions and when they are able to access their entitlements;
b has a high personal tax rate and is eligible to make salary sacrifice or personal contributions to reduce the tax payable;
c believes the investment earnings are likely to outperform, for example, interest rates on any borrowings loans; and
d is able to service debt.

Factors in favour of non-superannuation investments

A summary of the factors that would support investment outside the superannuation regime include where the member:

a is close to exceeding the limits imposed on contributions;
b wants to acquire investments which are of a value that the contributions caps would prevent the purchase;
c does not have any tax dependants—investing outside superannuation would allow those assets to pass tax free to non-dependants on the member's death;
d is looking to retire or otherwise have access savings prior to preservation age and therefore have access to investments earlier than permitted via superannuation;
e finds the superannuation laws, particularly in relation to SMSFs, unduly complex and subject to change too frequently;
f wants to invest with related parties without any restriction.

SMSF PDS

Summary

Purpose of PDS

This summary is designed to help you make a decision about whether to acquire an interest in an SMSF (**fund**).

The Law allows you 14 days from the date of issue of the PDS to decide if you wish to acquire an interest in the fund.

Information in a PDS

The PDS generally sets out:

(i) the nature of SMSF;

(ii) the main advantages and disadvantages of acquiring an interest in the fund; and

(iii) information about contributions, payment of benefits and related tax issues.

What you should do

If you decide to acquire an interest in the fund please sign and date the PDS.

Overview

This PDS is intended to be a general guide in relation to establishing and maintaining an SMSF. It is not intended to be legal or financial advice.

If you intend to take action (or not act) based on something dealt with in this PDS, you should firstly obtain specialist advice. Advice can generally be provided by any specialist financial adviser, accountant, or lawyer.

The PDS provides general commentary about SMSFs, including:

a their advantages and disadvantages;
b contributions;
c payment of benefits; and
d taxation issues.

SMSFs

An SMSF is a superannuation fund with four or less members established by a trust deed. The members of an SMSF have sole responsibility to manage the fund. In contrast, larger funds have an independent trustee who is responsible for all aspects of managing the fund.

Advantages and disadvantages

The main advantages and disadvantages of an SMSF, are outlined below.

The advantages of an SMSF can include:

- a trustees have the discretion to choose the investments of the fund, within its investment;
- b ability to borrow to buy assets;
- c generally a maximum 15% tax rate on income and a 10% tax rate on capital gains;
- d generally a 0% tax rate for members aged at least 60 receiving on income stream;
- e flexibility on tailoring how members receive benefits, including using TRIS;
- f complementary estate planning arrangements using benefit nominations;
- g flexibility in relation to insurance arrangements;
- h intergenerational wealth management (subject to the maximum member limit of 4 members);
- i tax-free payments when the member dies to their 'tax dependants' (explained below);
- j ability to transfer assets to members 'as is' (or 'in specie'), instead of being sold and the cash distributed;
- k asset protection on a member's bankruptcy;
- l reduced reporting requirements when compared with larger funds; and
- m ability to potentially access a lower fee structure than that for larger funds.

Depending on your circumstances, many of the advantages outlined above may in fact be disadvantages.

Some other specific disadvantages of an SMSF can include:

- a the amount of personal involvement, responsibility and specialised knowledge required to manage the fund;
- b fees can be greater than those for larger funds, particularly if the SMSF has a small asset base;
- c once established, it can be difficult to unwind an SMSF, particularly if its assets are illiquid; and
- d there are strict Australian residency rules for members.

Establishing an SMSF

The main steps to establish an SMSF are summarised below.

Trust deed

A document confirming the rules by which the trustee administers the SMSF must be prepared (trust deed). All trustees are bound by the trust deed and are jointly responsible for any breach of it.

The deed must be dated, signed by each trustee and updated regularly for changes in the law.

Trustee eligibility

An individual trustee, or a director of a corporate trustee must be:

a at least 18 years of age; and
b not an undischarged bankrupt, insane or a 'disqualified person'.

A person will be a 'disqualified person' if they are:

a insolvent;
b convicted of an offence relating to dishonest conduct at any time; or
c subject to a civil penalty order for breaches of the superannuation laws.

Trustees

The trustees manage the SMSF and must be either a company or individuals. For constitutional reasons where there are individual trustees, the purpose of the SMSF must be the provision of old age pensions.

A sole purpose company acting as trustee is generally seen as best practice as it:

a allows greater certainty and control because companies can exist indefinitely;
b gives access to lower annual ASIC lodgement fees as compared to other companies; and
c ensures fewer administrative costs when control of the SMSF changes. For example, the removal or admission of an individual trustee means title to each asset of the fund must be changed. For a corporate trustee, all that is required when changing a director is a notice to ASIC. Title in the assets of the fund remains in the name of the corporate trustee.

Election

To access the concessional taxation regime, the trustee of an SMSF must lodge an election with the ATO within 60 days of establishing the fund.

Applications for TFN, ABN and GST

Trustees must lodge an 'Application to Register for the New Tax System Superannuation Entity' form to obtain a TFN, ABN and, if necessary, to register for the GST.

Specific steps may also be required to ensure compliance with:

a PAYG obligations;
b withholding tax; and
c various state taxes.

Standards of care

There are a number of minimum standards of care imposed on every trustee of an SMSF, including acting:

a honestly;
b prudently;
c in the best interests of members; and
d in accordance with the standards of care prescribed under the superannuation laws.
e Any breach of these standards of care can trigger civil and criminal penalties.

Bank account

A trustee must establish a bank account to hold all money belonging to an SMSF separate from other accounts (for example from members, the trustee personally and from contributing employers).

Any cheques paid to an SMSF should be clearly marked, for example, 'XYZ Pty Ltd as trustee for the SMSF Fund'.

Any investments by an SMSF should be similarly recorded.

Remuneration

Trustees cannot be paid for performing their trustee duties in managing an SMSF.

Costs and cooling off period

Costs

There are numerous costs associated with operating an SMSF, including:

a legal fees establishing the fund;
b accounting fees in preparing regulatory returns and administering the fund;
c transaction costs in relation to acquiring and maintaining assets; and
d ongoing management costs (including audit fees on an annual basis).

The quantum of fees can vary between firms and best practice involves considering the likely costs prior to deciding to establish an SMSF.

Cooling off period

This PDS is designed to help you decide whether to acquire an interest in an SMSF.

The Law allows you 14 days from the date of issue of this PDS to decide if you want to proceed.

It is important to note that during this cooling off period you have the right to decide not to acquire an interest in an SMSF.

Trustee and member eligibility

Specific rules apply to admission as a trustee or member of an SMSF depending on issues such as whether the SMSF has:

a individual trustees;
b a corporate trustee; or
c is a single member fund.

Individual trustees

Where an SMSF has individual trustees:

a the fund can only have a maximum of four members;
b each individual trustee must be a member of the fund and vice versa; and
c no member can be an employee of another member of the fund, unless they are related.

Corporate trustee

Where an SMSF has a corporate trustee, essentially the same rules as those for an SMSF controlled by individual trustees apply, however each director of the trustee company must be a fund member and vice versa.

Single member

Where an SMSF has a single member, the SMSF must satisfy one of the following rules:

a it must have a corporate trustee of which the member is the sole director;
b it must have a corporate trustee of which the member is one of only two directors and the other director is either a relative, or a person who is not a relative and also not an employer, of the member; or
c two individual trustees, one of whom is the member and the other is either a relative, or a person who is not a relative and also not an employer, of the member.

Exceptions

The trustee and member rules are subject to the following main exceptions:

- a a parent or guardian can act as trustee or director for a member under 18;
- b where a member is deceased or incapacitated, a LPR can act as trustee for that member;
- c a beneficiary of a pension paid following a member's death is considered a member of the fund if that beneficiary is not already a member (and therefore must become a trustee or if the trustee is a company, a director of the trustee); and
- d a person holding an enduring power of attorney for an incapacitated member can act as a trustee or director for a member without formally being a member.

Investments

Sole purpose test

SMSFs must comply with the 'sole purpose test' in the SIS Act to avoid significant penalties.

This means all investment of the fund must be acquired for the sole purpose of providing retirement benefits for members and also comply with various investment rules.

Written investment strategy

Before acquiring any investment, an SMSF must have a written investment strategy taking into account issues such as cash flow, risk, return, diversification, liquidity and ability of the fund to meet liabilities when they arise.

The investment risk profiles of each individual member of the SMSF must also be considered. For example, it might be appropriate that members nearing retirement have a higher proportion of their funds invested in low risk, capital preserving investments.

A financial adviser or investment manager holding an Australian Financial Services Licence should be engaged if the trustee requires any guidance about an SMSF's investment strategy.

An SMSF investment strategy must be reviewed and updated regularly.

Types of investments

An SMSF can generally invest in any form of assets including shares, bonds, property, and cash. However speculative investments, even in traditional asset classes (for example share futures trading) may not be considered a prudent investment in the context of the 'sole purpose test' outlined above.

The ATO also generally considers certain 'lifestyle' related investments (for example, cars, boats, beach houses and artwork) that can be enjoyed, leased or used personally by fund members or their related parties as inappropriate investments.

Specialist advice should be obtained before investing in a manner that does not clearly align with the sole purpose test and an agreed investment strategy.

Restrictions on investments

There are a number of restrictions on the types of investments an SMSF may make. The main rules are set out below.

Overview

An SMSF cannot lend money or otherwise provide financial assistance to members or related parties.

An SMSF can only borrow money if:

- a the lender complies with the limited recourse loan provisions;
- b it relates to the settlement of share transactions within 7 days and the value of the transaction is less than 10% of the value of the fund;
- c the borrowing helps fund benefit payments and the amount borrowed is less than 10% of the value of the fund and is for less than 90 days.

An SMSF should ensure all transactions are on arm's length terms.

Specific constraints

An SMSF must ensure less than 5% of the market value of its assets are invested in IHAs. IHAs include investments in, loans to or a lease arrangement with a related party.

Related parties include fund members and their associates (such as relatives, business partners and entities controlled by a member or their associates).

Importantly, the prohibition on an SMSF acquiring assets from a member or a related party does not apply to:

- a listed shares;
- b business real property (as defined in the SIS Act);
- c interests in a widely held unit trust; or
- d interests in a closely held unit trust where there are no borrowings.

Specialist advice should be obtained before seeking access to any of the above exceptions.

Contributions

Contributions to an SMSF can generally be made by:

a an employer of a member;
b a member; and
c the spouse of the member.

The quantum of concessional contributions permitted in a financial year is subject to a limit for each employee that contributions are made for.

Concessional contributions which count towards the concessional limit include all employer contributions (e.g. super guarantee and salary sacrifice), member contributions which are claimed as a tax deduction and certain allocations from fund reserves.

The amount of non-concessional member contributions is also subject to annual limits.

All individuals under the age of 65, and those aged 65 to 74 who meet a work test, can claim a tax deduction for personal contributions to eligible superannuation funds up to the concessional contributions cap (explained below).

Under 65

As noted above, anyone under the age of 65 can make contributions without restrictions.

Between the ages of 65 and 74

Contributions from a person aged 65 to 74 can be made if the person has been gainfully employed on at least a part time basis during the financial year.

The specific definition in this regard is that the person worked at least 40 hours over a period of not more than 30 consecutive days in the financial year.

Over 75

A person cannot make personal superannuation contributions from 28 days after the end of the month in which they turn 75.

Under 18

Persons under the age of 18 are entitled to a deduction for contributions if they have derived income from the carrying on a business or from eligible employment.

Contribution limits

The maximum amount of concessional and non-concessional contributions that may be paid by an employer, a self-employed person or a member without potentially being subject to excess contributions tax, is set out below. This table represents the position on announcement from 1 July 2017. The government has committed to indexing these amounts:

Contribution type	Contribution limit
Concessional contributions	$25,000 per annum per person, regardless of age
Non-concessional contributions	$100,000 per annum per person, as long as the member has a member balance of less than $1.6MThere is also a 'bring forward' option. To access the non-concessional bring forward, the member must: (a) be younger than 65 years old for one day during the relevant year (the first year); (b) contribute more than the annual cap (ie more than $100,000); and (c) have a total super balance of less than $1.5million on 30June of the previous year. Where accessed, the bring forward rules provide that the remaining cap amount for the second or third year of a bring forward arrangement is reduced to zero if the total super balance of the member is greater than $1.6M on 30June of the previous financial year.

For any excess superannuation contributions breaching the non-concessional cap, the government will allow individuals to withdraw those excess contributions and associated earnings.

If a member chooses this option, no excess contributions tax will be payable and any related earnings will be taxed at their marginal tax rate.

As is well understood, concessional contributions to superannuation can generally be made by:

a an employer of a member;
b a member; and
c the spouse of the member.

The rules in relation to the quantum of permissible concessional contributions (historically referred to as deductible contributions) have been subject to regular change. The changes have primarily focused on the dollar limit for contributions made in each financial year.

Concessional contributions which currently count towards the annual concessional limit include:

a all employer contributions (e.g. super guarantee, salary sacrifice);
b member contributions which are claimed as a tax deduction; and
c in some situations, allocations from any fund reserves.

Contributions can be less than the maximum deductible contributions and any contributions made should be credited to a member's accumulation account within 28 days of the end of the month they are received.

From 1 July 2018 if an individual has a member balance of less than $500,000, they may use their unused concessional caps for a period of up to five years, and in effect make 'catch-up' concessional contributions.

Spouse contributions

Where a spouse is a member of the fund, eligible spouse contributions may be accepted by an SMSF at any time if the spouse is under the age of 65.

If the spouse is aged 65 to 74, eligible spouse contributions may only be accepted if the spouse is gainfully employed on at least a part time basis. If the spouse is 75 or over, no spouse contributions can be made.

Contributions for children under 18

Parents, grandparents, friends and employers can contribute on behalf of children.

Co-contribution for low income earners

If a person makes a personal super contribution, the Government will make a co-contribution up to certain limits. The thresholds change every year, as a guide, the amounts for the year ending on 30 June 2017 were as follows:

Lower income threshold	Higher income threshold	Co-contribution	Maximum entitlement
$36,021	$51,021	$0.50 for every $1, up to a maximum super co-contribution limit of $500 a year	The maximum entitlement is $500. However, this is reduced by 3.333 cents for every dollar of total income, less business deductions over $36,021, up to $51,021.

Minimum employer contributions

Employers must contribute a minimum amount of superannuation support for each employee as set out in the SG Act.

The minimum amount progressively contributed by an employer is 9% to 12% between 1 July 2012 and 1 July 2019. The rate is 9.5%from 1 July 2014 and will remain at this leveluntil at least 30 June 2021. The intention is that the rate will then increase by 0.5 percentage points each year until it reaches 12% in 2025/26.

Contributions on behalf of directors of corporate trustees

One further issue that often arises is whether the corporate trustee of a family trust can claim a tax deduction for the super contributions paid on behalf of a director to a complying superannuation fund?

A taxpayer is entitled to a deduction for a contribution it makes to a superannuation fund for the purpose of providing superannuation benefits for another person who is the taxpayer's employee when the contribution is made.

For this purpose, an employee includes both an individual who is either an employee under common law or an employee within the expanded meaning under the SG Act.

The expanded definition of 'employee' treats a person who is entitled to payment for the performance of duties as a member of an executive body (whether described as the board of directors or otherwise) of a body corporate as an employee of that body corporate in relation to those duties.

'Whether the director of a trustee company of a family trust is entitled to payment for performance of duties' will always ultimately be a question of fact in the particular circumstances.

Importantly, the actual payment for duties is not required, provided that the director is entitled to payment for performance of duties.

Where the director is an employee for these purposes, the deduction will only be available where three other conditions are satisfied. These are summarised below.

First, the member must be:

- a an employee of the employer within the expanded meaning;
- b engaged in producing the employer's assessable income; or
- c an Australian resident who is engaged in the employer's business.

Secondly, one of the following requirements must be satisfied:

- a the SMSF must be a complying superannuation fund;
- b at the time the taxpayer made the contribution, the taxpayer had reasonable grounds to believe that the SMSF was a complying superannuation fund; or
- c at or before the time the taxpayer made the contribution, the taxpayer obtained a written statement (given by or on behalf of the SMSF) that the fund:
    - (i) was a resident regulated superannuation fund (within the meaning of the SIS Act); and
    - (ii) was not subject to a direction under the SIS Act, which prevents a fund from accepting employer contributions.

Finally, a deduction will only be available in the circumstances where the taxpayer made the contribution on or before the date that is 28months after the end of the month in which the employee turns 75.

Payment of benefits

The SMSF established under most trust deeds (**Trust Deed**) is an allocated accumulation fund. This means the total amount of a member's accumulation account will be their entitlement in the fund on an access event.

The accumulation account is made up of all contributions, rollover payments and income on those amounts, less expenses and taxation.

Access events

Benefits are payable as either of, or a contribution of:

a a lump sum; or
b an income stream.

A number of rules apply to any income stream to be paid by the fund and specialist advice should be received before a member or beneficiary commences an income stream

The events which trigger access to benefits are:

a disability superannuation benefit—benefits are payable if a member has suffered physical or mental ill health and the member is unlikely to be gainfully employed again in a position for which the member is reasonably qualified due to their education, experience or training;
b retirement—once the preservation age is attained (explained below) a retirement following that date triggers access to benefits
c early retirement from employment—benefits can become payable on early retirement from employment;
d death—benefits must be paid on the death of a member; and
e TRIS—there can be access to a non commutable income stream upon attaining the relevant preservation age (as from 1 July 2017, income generated from assets supporting the payment of the TRIS will be taxed at 15%).

Preserved benefits

The Government requires preservation of benefits until a member retires from the workforce on or after attaining the preservation age subject to exceptions such as total and permanent disablement or a TRIS.

The preservation age is 60, subject to the following exceptions:

Date of Birth	Preservation Age
After 30 June 1964	60
Between 30 June 1963 and 1 July 1964	59
Between 30 June 1962 and 1 July 1963	58
Between 30 June 1961 and 1 July 1962	57
Between 30 June 1960 and 1 July 1961	56
Before 1 July 1960	55

Generally, all benefits in a superannuation fund must be preserved until the member's preservation age. There are some limited exceptions to this rule, and again specialist advice should be sought before seeking to gain early access.

Death benefits

Where a member dies their benefit must be paid to:

a a superannuation dependant (essentially an immediate family member); or
b the member's LPR.

A beneficiary who is a superannuation dependant may also not qualify as a dependant for tax purposes (known as a 'tax dependant').

A tax dependant of deceased member includes only:

a any spouse;
b former spouse;
c any children under the age of 18; and
d any other person who was dependant upon or had an interdependency relationship with the deceased.

Tax will generally be payable on any benefits distributed other than to tax dependants.

The taxation consequences also differ depending on whether the amount is paid as a lump sum or an income stream and, in the case of an income stream, the ages of the deceased person and the recipient.

Only tax dependants can receive an income stream.

BDBNs

The trust deed permits BDBNs whereby a member can direct the trustee to pay their benefits on death to nominated dependants.

The BDBN can also specify the manner in which the member's benefit is to be paid (that is lump sum or an income stream or both).

Advantages of BDBNs

Three of the main advantages of BDBNs are:

- a reduced risk of successful disputes over death benefit payments;
- b tax planning opportunities for member's with infant children; and
- c asset protection planning.

Disadvantages of BDBNS

Three of the main disadvantages of BDBNs are:

- a the tax and estate planning issues in relation to the payment of superannuation death benefits are complex and difficulties can often arise with BDBNs that prove to be inappropriate;
- b if a member's circumstances change and they have failed to update their BDBN, the original BDBN will remain binding on the trustee; and
- c a number of court decisions since 2012 have resulted in significant confusion about the exact requirements to ensure a BDBN is valid.

Members may also implement standard nominations (or non-BDBN), which give the trustee guidance as to where to pay a benefit, but need not be followed.

Taxation

Tax on payments

Benefits distributed to a member will be taxed either as a:

- a Tax Free Component; or
- b Taxable Component.

As the tax regime is complex, specialist advice should be sought, however broadly the position is as follows:

Lump sums	Age or dependant status	Tax treatment (Tax Rate %)	
		Tax Free Component	Taxable Component
Paid from a super fund	Under 55	0%	20%
	55 to 59	0%	Up to low rate threshold: 0% Balance: 15%
	60 and over	0%	0%
Death benefit	Tax dependant	0%	0%
	Non-tax dependant	0%	15%, or 30% on certain insured benefits
Pensions	**Age**		**Tax treatment**
Paid from super fund	55 to 59	0%	[Taxable component x marginal tax rate] –15% rebate
	60 and over	0%	0%
Death pension—reversionary pension paid to tax dependant (RB) of a primary beneficiary (PB) on death	PB < 60 and RB < 60	0%	[Taxable component x marginal tax rate] –15% rebate
	PB < 60 and RB > 60	0%	0%
	PB > 60	0%	0%

The low rate threshold is $195,000 for the 2016/2017 financial year. This amount is reduced by any amount previously applied to the low rate threshold.

Where benefits have not been subject to contributions tax in the fund (i.e. there is an element untaxed in the fund), an untaxed plan cap applies. This cap is set at $1,415,000 for the 2016/2017 financial year.

The ATO confirms updates to these amounts periodically.

Rollovers

If a member's benefits are rolled over into another superannuation fund, approved deposit fund or annuity, no tax is payable until they ultimately receive the benefit.

Concessional contributions

Concessional contributions are sourced from pre-tax income. If a contribution is made within the concessional contribution limit it is taxable in the hands of the trustee at 15%. Any contributions above the concessional contribution limit trigger an additional tax of 31.5% on top of the 15%.

Non-concessional contributions

Non-concessional contributions are sourced from after tax income. Personal non concessional contributions within the non-concessional contribution limit are not subject to tax.

Non-concessional contributions above the non-concessional contribution limit are taxed at the top marginal rate of 46.5%, plus Medicare levy.

Low income spouse offset

An income tax rebate of up to $540 per annum is available to a person who makes a superannuation contribution to a complying superannuation fund on behalf of a low or no income spouse under the age of 70 years (although the work test must be met for spouses aged between 65-69).

To qualify for the rebate a number of conditions must be satisfied including:

a contributions must be from after tax income; and
b the spouse's assessable income must be less than $40,000.

Income tax

The standard tax rate for an SMSF is 15%.

The effective tax rate may be less than 15% due to imputation credits paid to an SMSF.

When franking rebates exceed the 15% rate, an SMSF can use the excess to offset its tax liability on other income.

An SMSF is also entitled to a refund of excess imputation credits if there is no other assessable income (and therefore no tax liability) to take advantage of the excess rebate.

However 'special' income is taxed at 46.5%. Special income includes:

a income where the fund and the other entity are not dealing with each other at arm's length; and
b certain trust distributions (from discretionary or unit trusts) where the distributions are not at arm's length.

Deductions

General rules for deductions apply to SMSFs. This means that fund expenses are deductible to the extent to which they are incurred in gaining or producing assessable income.

Some expenses of an SMSF which are generally deductible include:

a administration fees;
b actuarial costs;
c accountancy and audit fees;

d costs of providing death or disability benefits such as insurance premiums; and

e investment adviser fees.

CGT

A one-third discount applies on any capital gain an SMSF realises if the asset has been owned for more than 12 months.

Subject to strict rules, the small business CGT retirement exemption of $500,000 from the sale of an 'active business asset' by a member can be rolled into an SMSF.

GST

Generally the investment activities of an SMSF do not have GST consequences. However, certain transactions may constitute taxable supplies, in which case the SMSF must collect GST and remit it to the ATO.

One example relates to limited recourse borrowing arrangements (explained later in this book). In this regard the ATO's position is that the borrowing trust is in essence a bare trust of which the SMSF is the absolutely entitled beneficiary.

Therefore the ATO adopts a 'look through' approach in considering the relevant entity that is 'carrying on the enterprise.' The ATO recognises that in bare trust arrangements the beneficiary (that is the SMSF) is usually the entity making the ultimate supply or acquisition.

This means the SMSF in a borrowing trust arrangement is usually the entity that is required to be registered for GST given it is the entity that is 'carrying on the enterprise' for the purpose of acquiring the relevant enterprise.

Other information

Annual statement

The trustee should issue an annual statement to each member confirming their current entitlements in the fund.

Deed variation

The trust deed allows the trustee to vary the trust deed.

However, any variation cannot reduce the accrued benefits of a member without the consent of that member unless the reduction is required to enable the fund to continue to comply with legislative requirements.

Medical evidence

The trust deed allows the trustees to effect insurance for death and disability.

The insurance company that undertakes the insurance may require certain information about a member's medical condition before allowing the trustee to obtain a policy.

Expenses

Various expenses of operating an SMSF can be debited as the trustee determines against the members' accumulation accounts, including:

a the costs of any insurance policy or annuity;
b tax on contributions, investment earnings or other fund income or benefits payments;
c administrative expenses including the costs of preparing and lodging the annual ATO returns; and
d investment losses.

Forfeiture

The trust deed allows a member's benefits to be forfeited in certain circumstances, including:

a on an attempted assignment or charge of a benefit; and
b where in the opinion of the trustee any fraud, embezzlement or serious misconduct as a member have occurred.

Upon forfeiture, the entitlement can be dealt with as the trustee determines.

For obvious reasons, there are extremely strict provisions that must be followed before a member's entitlement can be forfeited and specialist advice should always be obtained.

Subject to certain criteria, a member's benefits are however protected from the claims of creditors in the event of bankruptcy or insolvency.

In particular, a member's entitlement in an SMSF, while they remain in accumulation mode, will generally be protected on bankruptcy, with no dollar limit to this level of protection.

Winding up funds

The trust deed allows for the fund to be wound up.

An SMSF can be wound up at any time.

Specialist advice should be obtained before winding up an SMSF, as there are a range of issues to be addressed including:

a taxation, stamp duty and other costs on the transfer of assets;
b complying with the trust deed;

c discharging all liabilities, outstanding tax and charges;
d preparation and lodgement of tax and regulatory returns and notifications; and
e potentially deregistering any corporate trustee.

Non compliance

If an SMSF is deemed by the ATO to be non-complying then the following taxation consequences generally arise:

a for every year that the SMSF remains non-complying, its assessable income is taxed at highest marginal tax rate;
b in the year that it becomes non-complying, it includes in its assessable income an amount equal to the market value of the SMSFs total assets (less any contributions the fund has received that are not part of the taxable income of the fund);
c the pension exemption is not available;
d a general interest charge is also usually payable, which can be significant where the ATO issues the notice of non-compliance in respect of a financial year from many years earlier.

The ATO has confirmed that it will consider the following factors when deciding whether to issue an SMSF with a notice of non-compliance:

a The tax consequences in making an SMSF non-complying and the financial impacts this would have on the members of the fund;
b The seriousness of the contravention, including:
    (i) trustee's behaviour;
    (ii) the effect the contravention has on the SMSF's assets; and
    (iii) the number and duration of contraventions.

c All other relevant circumstances, including:
    (i) if the trustee has rectified the contravention;
    (ii) the level of skill and knowledge of the trustee;
    (iii) the compliance history of the fund; and
    (iv) the events which led to the contravention.

Generally the ATO argues that its main focus is encouraging SMSF trustees to comply with the superannuation laws, and therefore it will prefer to utilise one of the following approaches, rather than make a fund non-complying:

a trustee education and direction;
b enforceable undertakings;
c rectification direction;
d administrative penalties;
e disqualification of a particular trustee (or director of a corporate trustee;
f civil and criminal penalties;

g allowing the SMSF to be wound up; and
h temporary freezing of an SMSF's assets.

Is the trust deed up to date?

Difficulties can arise if an SMSF trust deed is not up to date and compliant with the law and planning strategies.

Any deficiency in the trust deed could result in there being substantial extra tax to pay, a severe lack of flexibility and possibly certain trustee decisions being rendered invalid. In an estate-planning context, some of the issues that should be considered include whether:

a the deed permits the making of a BDBN;
b there are any restrictions in relation to BDBNs (assuming they are permitted)—for instance, whom they may be paid to, whether the benefit is to be paid as a lump sum or as a pension, or whether there are time limits within which the death benefit is to be paid;
c the deed permits a broad range of benefit options, including lump sum benefits, pensions and a mixture of both. The deed should also authorise reversionary pensions—that is, allowing the member's pension to be paid to the member's dependants upon the member's death;
d the deed complies with current legislative provisions;
e the deed allows for individual and/or corporate trustees, as desired;
f benefits can be paid out in kind;
g in kind contributions can be made; and
h eligible spouse contributions can be made.

Generally, in the absence of the need to be prescriptive in specific areas, SMSF trust deeds should be drafted so as to be as flexible as possible.

Age of trust deed

The age of the trust deed is generally a significant determinant of whether it should be updated. Specifically, there are some critical dates which, if the trust deed were established, or the most recent amendment occurred, prior to that date then serious consideration should be given as to whether the trust deed needs updating.

The superannuation system, as a whole, changed considerably with the introduction of the SIS Act. Generally speaking, trust deeds established prior to that date should be updated. SMSFs which still have trust deeds executed prior to that date raise additional concerns about how the fund obtained a notification that it is a complying fund—that is, a fund that complies with the provisions of the SIS Act and which requires an election by the fund trustee that the SIS Act applies to the SMSF.

Further significant amendments to the SIS Act were made in 2003 with, among other things, the introduction of the co-contribution rules.

Spouse contribution splitting was introduced on 1 January 2006 before the simplified super reforms came into force on 1 July 2007. The simplified super changes were arguably the most comprehensive changes since the introduction of the SIS Act and included:

a changes to the taxation of eligible termination payments;
b changes to the payment of death benefits;
c the abolition of reasonable benefit limits and the introduction of the contributions caps.

Further significant changes were introduced as part of the 2016 Federal Budget (with most commencing on 1 July 2017), including:

a Introduction of a $1.6Mtransfer balance cap for retirement;
b Removal of the tax exemption for TRIS;
c Reduction in the annual concessional (before-tax) contributions cap to $25,000;
d Enabling unused concessional contributions to brought forward for a period of up to 5 years provided a member's balance is less than $500,000;
e Reduction in the annual non-concessional (after-tax) contributions cap to $100,000; and
f Removal of anti-detriment provisions.

Deeds of variation

Superannuation trust deeds can be totally revoked and replaced with a completely new document, while changes to a family trust deed tend to be extremely piecemeal.

The issue can be largely answered by reference to the Tax Office's approach to resettlements.

Broadly, the Tax Office accepts that in relation to superannuation funds, a resettlement for tax purposes will never occur. Due to this approach (and stamp duty exemptions that apply in essentially every Australian state), most advisers recommend that when updating a superannuation trust deed, it is best to adopt a completely new deed.

In contrast, where updating a family trust deed, because of the risks associated from a resettlement perspective, it is usually best to only amend the provisions that are in particular need of being addressed.

Some SMSF trust deed providers offer an 'automatic update' online.

Pensions and commutation

When reviewing the pension and commutation provisions of a deed, ideally the terms of a trust deed should be as flexible as possible and allow the payment of all types of pensions.

Some older deeds are particularly prescriptive in relation to the payment of pensions, this appears to have arisen on the basis that the SIS Regulations require that the rules for the payment of each type of pension ensure that certain prescribed conditions are met.

The prescriptive approach seems to have been adopted in older deeds as it was assumed that, if the rules for the payment of each type of pension were not set out clearly in the trust deed, and pensions were not paid in accordance with these rules, the requirement to ensure that pensions were paid in a particular way could not be met and the SIS Regulations would be contravened.

However, the governing rules of an SMSF include not only the terms of the trust deed but also any rules contained in other documentation and any unwritten rules.

Therefore, the more modern approach is to have the pension provisions in the trust deed drawn as flexibly as possible.

As noted above, there is a $1.6M (subject to indexation for inflation) transfer cap for each member of an SMSF. This amount is a limit on the capital value a member may have to support a pension.

This means that the income generated on assets supporting a pension within the $1.6M cap is tax free. In contrast, income generated on assets above the gap will be taxed in the same manner as a member in accumulation phase—that is at a flat rate of 15%.

The amount of the gap used is not adjusted due for withdrawals from the fund or if the underlying assets lose value. The cap may however be adjusted due to:

- a commutations back to accumulation phase;
- b payments as a result of a family law settlement;
- c court orders; or
- d payments made due to bankruptcy.

In addition, amounts received by the beneficiary of a reversionary pension will generally be counted towards that beneficiary's transfer cap, subject to some modifications for children.

Reserves

In relation to reserve accounts, it is generally recommended that the trust deed provide for the creation of reserve accounts. This is particularly important in relation to excess contributions.

Re-contribution strategy

Any savings (and any earnings on these savings) held within superannuation that are 'tax-free components' are able to be distributed tax-free on death.

Tax-free components include:

a non-concessional contributions (formerly referred to as 'un-deducted contributions'), where no tax deduction has been received in relation to amounts contributed (for example, contributions made from post-tax earnings); and
b government co-contributions.

One strategy that was historically of benefit involved withdrawing the taxable component from superannuation and then re-contributing it as a non-concessional contribution, with the result that all benefits became tax-free and enabled the whole super benefit to be paid to non-dependants as a lump sum, tax-free on a member's death.

Since 1 July 2007, and due to further changes in 2017, the usefulness of this strategy has been weakened because:

a any withdrawal from an SMSF on a lump sum basis must be made proportionately as between tax-free and taxable components. In other words, it is not possible to withdraw only the taxable component;
b there are significant limitations placed on the ability to contribute tax-free components to superannuation, as outlined in chapter 1 of this book

An alternative strategy that has developed is the establishment of an additional SMSF to receive all non-concessional contributions (tax-free components) so that, upon the member's death, the whole super benefit is paid to non-dependants, with the vast majority of that benefit being tax-free (although any earnings from investing the tax-free component are taxable). For example, the member could contribute any pension payments received or any after-tax amounts to the newly established SMSF.

Chapter 2

INVESTMENT BORROWING STRUCTURES

Overview

Generally, the trustee of an SMSF is prevented from borrowing money or maintaining an existing borrowing, unless the trustee complies with provisions of section 67A of the SIS Act.

It is important to note that, notwithstanding the borrowing might otherwise comply with the limited recourse borrowing provisions in section 67A of the SIS Act, there must be a specific power for the trustee to borrow, contained in the trust deed.

Furthermore, most financiers will require a number of other specific powers in the trust deed including:

a the power to grant the security for the borrowing;
b the power to instruct the trustee of the trust which is to hold the asset that is the subject of the borrowing;
c the ability for the SMSF trustee to be indemnified out of the assets of the SMSF, in the event the financier takes action;
d the ability to accept various types of contributions, which will be used by the SMSF trustee to make the repayments on the borrowing; and
e the power to grant a power of attorney to provide to the financier the ability to act on behalf of the fund, in the event of default.

Other than the limited recourse borrowing provisions in section 67A of the SIS Act, the main way an SMSF can potentially borrow is investing via a geared unit trust.

Limited recourse borrowing arrangements

In summary, a limited recourse borrowing trust structure ensures that:

a any asset acquired by the borrowing trust is held by the trustee on trust for the SMSF;
b the SMSF has the sole beneficial interest in all of the assets of the borrowing trust; and
c the SMSF has a right, by making one or more payments to the lender (**Lender**), to acquire legal ownership of all of the assets in the borrowing trust.

Any investment by the SMSF should comply with the investment rules prescribed by the SIS Act and SIS Regulations (together referred to as the **Law**), in particular, sections 67A and 67B if it meets the following criteria:

a the SMSF has borrowed money from the Lender which it has applied to acquire an original asset or a replacement asset (**Asset**) which the SMSF is permitted to acquire;
b the rights of the Lender as against the SMSF are of a limited recourse nature against the SMSF's interest in the Asset; and
c the Asset is the only asset held by the trustee of the limited recourse borrowing trust on trust for the SMSF.

Relevant investment rules

Prohibition on borrowings

Section 67(1) of the SIS Act contains a general prohibition against SMSFs borrowing, however, section 67A of the SIS Act allows borrowing in a narrow range of circumstances.

Limited recourse borrowing arrangements

An SMSF may borrow where the:

- a money is used to acquire an Asset that the trustee is permitted under the law to acquire (**first requirement**);
- b Asset is held on trust so that the trustee acquires a beneficial interest in the Asset (**second requirement**);
- c trustee has a right to acquire legal ownership of the Asset by making one or more payments (**third requirement**);
- d rights of the Lender (or any other person) against the trustee for default on the borrowing are limited to rights relating to the Asset (**fourth requirement**); and
- e rights of the Lender (or any other person) against the trustee for the trustee's exercise of any rights it may have are limited to rights relating to the Asset (**fifth requirement**).

Further comments in relation to each of the above requirements are set out in turn below.

First requirement

The SMSF must ensure that any borrowing is applied for the acquisition of a single acquirable asset. The asset must be one which the SMSF is permitted under the Law to acquire.

Some examples of assets that an SMSF can acquire include:

- a business real property (even if it is owned by a related party);
- b listed shares (even if it is owned by a related party);
- c residential property (although not if it is not owned by a related party); and
- d a collection of assets that have the same market value and are identical to each other.

Advice should be obtained before an SMSF acquires an asset not listed above to ensure it is in accordance with the Law.

One example of the potential risks in this regard is where three lots of a property are to be acquired simultaneously. In this situation, if each of the three lots can be sold and dealt with separately, the ATO is likely to treat each lot as a distinct asset.

The fact that the property may be used as a single commercial space, even if there are no dividing walls, does not change this outcome.

In this type of situation it would therefore be necessary for three separate borrowing trusts to be established (that is, one for each lot), together with three separate loans to be made and, ideally, three separate contracts of sale.

This said, in some limited circumstances, the ATO accepts that property held on multiple titles can be a single acquirable asset (e.g. if a factory is built across a number of lots such that the lots cannot be used or dealt with separately).

In particular, the ATO in SMSFR 2012/1 confirms that where more than one real property lot is being acquired, the property will be a 'single acquirable asset' where there is a:

- a unifying physical object, such as a permanent fixture which extends across two or more lots; or
- b requirement at law that the lots are dealt with together, for instance where water rights attach to a particular lot.

There are some exceptions to this rule, such as where multiple identical assets are being acquired (e.g. 100 shares in a listed company).

Importantly however, the SIS Act does not prevent the acquisition of multiple lots of land. Rather, it prevents an SMSF from borrowing to acquire multiple lots (unless a separate trust is established for each lot).

SMSFR 2012/1 makes it clear that the relevant prohibitions apply to the asset that is acquired at settlement of the contract. For instance, in relation to the prohibition on an SMSF borrowing to improve an asset, the ATO gives the following example:

> '*A similar outcome results if the contract is entered into for the purchase of a single title vacant block of land along with the constructions of a house on that land before settlement occurs. In this situation, the deposit paid upon entering into the contract and the balance payable upon settlement is applied for the acquisition, under that contract, of land with a completed house on it. The deposit and the balance payable at settlement may be funded under a single limited recourse borrowing arrangement.*'

Second requirement

The trustee of the borrowing trust will hold any asset on trust for the SMSF and the trust deed provides that the SMSF has a beneficial interest in each asset as the sole beneficiary.

Third requirement

The Trust Deed provides the SMSF with a right to acquire the legal ownership of any asset held via the limited recourse borrowing trust by making one or more payments.

Fourth requirement

The rights of the Lender (or any other person) against the SMSF trustee for default on the borrowing are usually contained in the loan establishment documents and must be limited to rights relating to the Asset, such that the Lender has limited recourse against the interest held by the SMSF.

Fifth requirement

If the SMSF has rights relating to the Asset (other than a right to acquire legal ownership by making one or more payments), the arrangements must be structured so that the rights of the Lender or any other person against the SMSF trustee for that trustee's exercise of its rights are limited to rights relating to the Asset.

Conclusion

If all five conditions are satisfied, then the SMSF can borrow from the Lender to acquire the Asset.

Borrowings

There are no rules about who the Lender can be, such that the Lender can be the member, or a party related to the member.

The wider provisions of the Law continue to apply in relation to the SMSF trustee and its investment decisions, including that all arrangements must be at arm's length.

The loan between the SMSF trustee and the Lender must reflect market conditions for similar arrangements, including the interest rate, rate of repayment, any defaulting rate of interest and the term of the loan.

For a period of time there was a view (supported by the ATO) that related party loans did not in fact need to be on arm's lengths terms in relation to the interest rate applied.

In Practical Compliance Guidelines (**PCG**) 2016/5 the ATO confirmed its view regarding interest rates for related party loans as part of an SMSF's limited recourse borrowing arrangements.

Broadly the ATO requires that where a related party borrowing is supported by a mortgage over real property in favour of the lender:

a the borrower must pay interest on the loan amount to the Lender monthly, calculated at the Reserve Bank of Australia (**RBA**) Indicator Lending Rate

A trustee of an SMSF intending on entering into a limited recourse borrowing arrangement should specifically ensure that:

a the SMSF obtains further legal advice if it intends to acquire an asset not clearly within the permitted investments for SMSFs; and
b any loan documentation limits the rights of the Lender (or any other person) against the SMSF trustee:
   (i) for default on the borrowing; or
   (ii) for the SMSF trustee's exercise of its rights relating to the Asset,

   to rights relating to the Asset as outlined above.

SMSF borrowing arrangements and business succession

Where more than one SMSF is involved with borrowing trust, the business succession arrangements should be carefully considered.

The main approaches, noting that the preferable solution depends on the exact commercial circumstances are as follows:

a As the intention with the borrowing arrangements is normally that they are self-funded, some clients choose to leave the structure in place and have an unfunded agreement (for example, a unit holder's agreement) regulating how the parties will conduct themselves if one of the principals passes away. In other words, the deceased's estate would treat the ownership interest in the building as an arm's length investment and would effectively maintain that interest until the other principal had sufficient funds to acquire the interest, or alternatively, the entire property was sold to a third party;
b Each principal can self-own insurance to pay out any debt referable to their interest in the underlying property. Having done this, the arrangement can then proceed essentially along the same lines as set out above;
c Each principal can obtain sufficient insurance to clear the entire debt. The buy-sell arrangement would require that 50% of the proceeds are paid to each principal (or their estate). The underlying property can then be dealt with as set out above, or alternatively, steps can also be taken to ensure that the property is transferred to the surviving principal's benefit, although the involvement of superannuation funds does create additional complications;
d A final alternative where there is only one SMSF involved utilises cross owned insurance policies. In business succession arrangements, cross owned insurance policies are rarely, if ever, utilised. Avoiding the use of cross owned policies is driven by a range of commercial reasons and the fact that invariably adverse tax consequences are unnecessarily triggered as the desired commercial outcomes can normally be achieved utilising self-owned policies that almost always deliver favourable tax outcomes;

Where an SMSF has a limited recourse borrowing trust arrangement in place to acquire an asset which forms a substantial part of the total value of the fund, cross owned policies historically have been seen to be very useful.

An example of how this approach (which historically had been given in principle support by the ATO) can work is as follows:

a The SMSF establishes a borrowing trust and borrows funds from a third party to acquire an asset;
b The (say) only two members of an SMSF are concerned that on the death of one of them, the ability to pay out the member's entitlement may be impossible to achieve without selling the underlying asset (i.e. neither member's account balance is large enough to represent the entire value of the acquired asset);
c If the members took out self-owned insurance policies, this would obviously not assist, given that the exiting member would effectively be entitled to an even greater share of the total assets of the fund;
d In contrast, if permissible under the trust deed for the SMSF, if cross owned policies are implemented, then the remaining member's balance would be the one that increases and the cash from the insurance policy could be used to pay the death benefit, while the continuing member would effectively have their member balance represented entirely by the asset originally acquired via the borrowing trust.

How exactly to structure this style of arrangement always depends on the particular circumstances. Great care should however be taken with the approach as, despite strong criticism from many specialist advisers, the ATO is on record as saying this style of strategy is not permissible in its view.

Insurance funded business succession generally

For many years, the ownership of insurance policies for business succession buy-sell arrangements through an SMSF has been popular, at least anecdotally. A detailed analysis of business succession is outside the scope of this book, however the author has published a book titled 'The Seven Foundations of Business Succession'.

In broad terms, primary advantages of business succession insurance policy ownership via an SMSF include:

a the premiums in relation to the insurance policies are normally deductible, 'freeing up' money outside the superannuation environment that would otherwise be needed to fund insurance premiums;
b the insurance proceeds can often be utilised within the SMSF to generate tax effective income streams via pensions; and

c BDBNs (whether lapsing or non-lapsing) can be used to ensure that the proceeds from the policy pass as intended by the exiting partner.

In deciding whether or not to structure insurance ownership through an SMSF, there are numerous issues that need to be considered, including:

a the impact of contribution limits, which can significantly undermine the usefulness of the strategy in many situations;
b whether there are circumstances surrounding the structure, which might jeopardise the ability of the SMSF to satisfy the sole purpose test, set out under the SIS Act. The ATO has publically flagged this as an issue, presumably where an SMSF has few, if any, other investment activities; and
c whether the arrangements are likely to fall foul of the general anti-avoidance provisions under part IVA of the Tax Act.

Historically the ATO has confirmed in various private documents that, when structured appropriately, an SMSF can own an insurance policy designed to assist the funding of a buy-sell arrangement, without breaching any tax or superannuation laws. In ATOID 2015/10 however the Tax Office confirmed its view that business succession insurance arrangements via an SMSF breach both the sole purpose test and financial assistance prohibition under the SIS Act.

It should also be remembered that the $1.6M transfer balance cap for retirement is likely to undermine the effectiveness of this style of strategy.

Example—Bank funding—limited recourse secured over property and other personal assets

The members of the SMSF offer their personal assets or act as a guarantor to provide additional security to the bank to secure the borrowing by the SMSF.

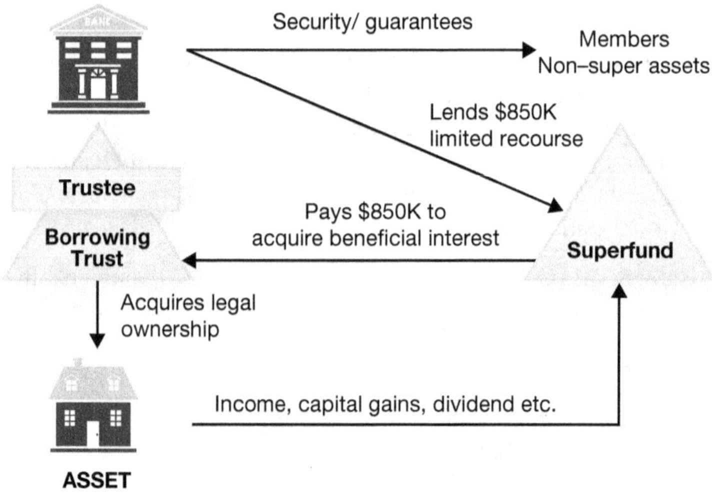

Bank funding—limited recourse secured over property

The SMSF is able to secure the borrowing from the bank without any member of the SMSF offering their personal assets or acting as a guarantor.

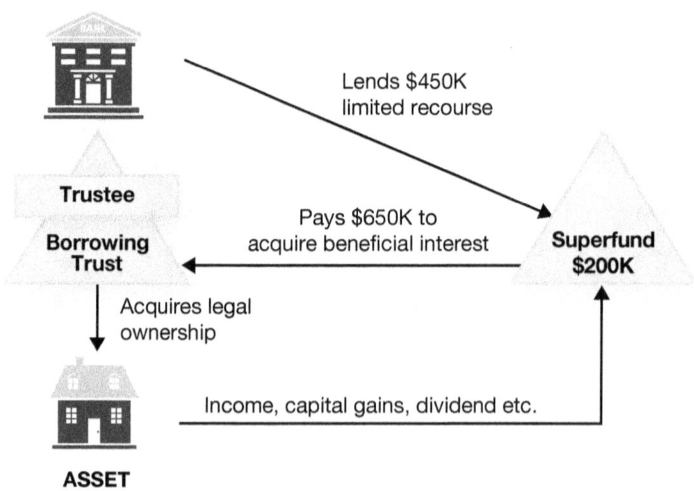

Self-funded—limited recourse secured over property

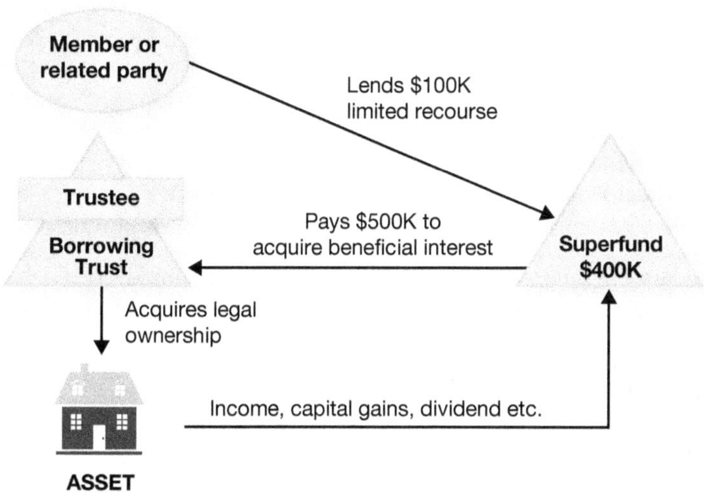

Geared Unit Trusts

Where a trust is not a 'related trust' under the SIS Act, then SMSFs can invest in it, even if the trust is geared, subject to certain rules, including:

a the trust deed for the SMSF permits the acquisition;
b the SMSF continues to comply with the SIS Act and SIS Regulations, particularly the sole purpose test; and
c the investment strategy for that SMSF justifies the basis on which the investment is made.

As set out below, generally an SMSF cannot invest in a related trust of the fund to an extent greater than 5% of the market value of the fund's total assets due to the IHA rules.

If an SMSF has IHAs with a value of more than 5% of the market value of the fund's total assets, then a range of penalties can be imposed by the ATO.

A geared trust should however not be a 'related trust' of an SMSF (and therefore not required to comply with the IHA rules) if it is structured so that:

a no one unitholder (including when grouped with 'related parties') can be entitled to more than 50% of the capital or income of the trust;
b no one unitholder (including when grouped with 'related parties') can control the trustee of the trust; or
c no one unitholder (including when grouped with 'related parties') can have the ability to unilaterally change the trustee of the trust.

Furthermore, any contractual arrangements between the unitholders (such as a unitholders agreement) must ensure that no aspect of the above prohibitions is breached.

Related parties

The SIS Act sets out who is a related party of an SMSF as follows:

a a member of the fund;
b a standard employer-sponsor of the fund; or
c a 'Part 8 associate' of a member or standard employer-sponsor.

A 'standard employer-sponsor' is defined as being an employer who contributes to an SMSF.

A Part 8 associate of a member is defined as including:

a their relatives;
b other members of the SMSF and trustees or directors of the trustee of the SMSF;
c the member's partners and partners' spouses or children ('partners' in this context refers to tax and general law partnerships, not life partners);
d a trustee of a trust that the member or a member and their related parties control; and
e a company that is sufficiently influenced by, or a majority voting interest is held by the member or a member and their related parties.

Best practice dictates that each aspect of the key tests must be reviewed carefully before an SMSF proceeds to invest in a geared unit trust.

Under section 70E (2) of the SIS Act, an entity will 'control' a trust if:

a a group in relation to the entity has a fixed entitlement to more than 50% of the capital or income of the trust;
b the trustee of the trust, or a majority of the trustees of the trust, is accustomed to or under an obligation (formal or informal) or might reasonably be expected to act in accordance with directions, instructions or wishes of a group in relation to the entity (whether those directions, instructions or wishes are, or might reasonably be expected to be, communicated directly or through interposed companies, partnerships or trusts); or
c a group in relation to the entity is able to remove or appoint the trustee, or a majority of the trustees.

Section 70E (3) of the SIS Act defines a 'group' to mean:

a the entity acting alone;
b a Part 8 associate of the entity acting alone;
c the entity and one or more Part 8 associates of the entity acting together; or
d two or more Part 8 associates of the entity acting together.

What does 'sufficiently influenced' mean?

The concept of whether a director is 'sufficiently influenced' by other persons is always one of the most important issues that needs to be resolved before an SMSF proceeds with this style of arrangement.

Generally, a director will be considered to be sufficiently influenced by a third party where they act in accordance with that other party's directions or wishes.

While the concept is relatively easy to define, its application in any specific factual scenario will almost always depend on an interpretation of the circumstances.

Some examples of where a director has been held to be sufficiently influenced by another person includes:

a A husband and wife (who were the only directors of a company) have been held to be influenced by their sons, because they never made any substantive decision without consultation with the sons and their intention was to ultimately appoint the sons as directors.

b A company has been held to be controlled solely by one director, even when there was an independent third party as a co-director, because the third party had no input into the management of the company and had simply been appointed to create the impression that the board was independent.

c A sole director company, where the director was an independent appointment, was held to be controlled by the ultimate shareholders of the company, as the director simply acted in accordance with the directions of the shareholders.

Ultimately, the ATO has confirmed that it is necessary to take into account all of the evidence and conduct between parties and the concept of a party 'significantly influencing' a third party will exist where it can be said to be likely that the other party would act in accordance with the wishes expressed.

Section 71(4)—deemed IHA

Even where the technical provisions outlined above are satisfied, there is a potential risk that the ATO may review such an investment or arrangement and apply the 'catch-all' provision for IHAs contained in section 71(4) of the SIS Act.

Section 71(4) of the SIS Act extends the application of the IHA rule by providing that the ATO may determine that a loan or investment of an SMSF, or an asset subject to a lease or lease arrangement should be deemed to be an IHA even where it would otherwise fall outside the IHA tests in section 71 of the SIS Act.

Breach of IHA rules

It should also be noted that the IHA rules are subject to the civil penalty provisions under section 84(1) of the SIS Act and trustees of SMSFs may be subject to penalties where the rules are breached.

Specifically, a breach of the IHA rules will usually result in an SMSF losing complying fund status and entitlement to tax concessions.

However, a contravention of the IHA rules will not affect the validity of the transaction.

Example structure of a geared unit trust

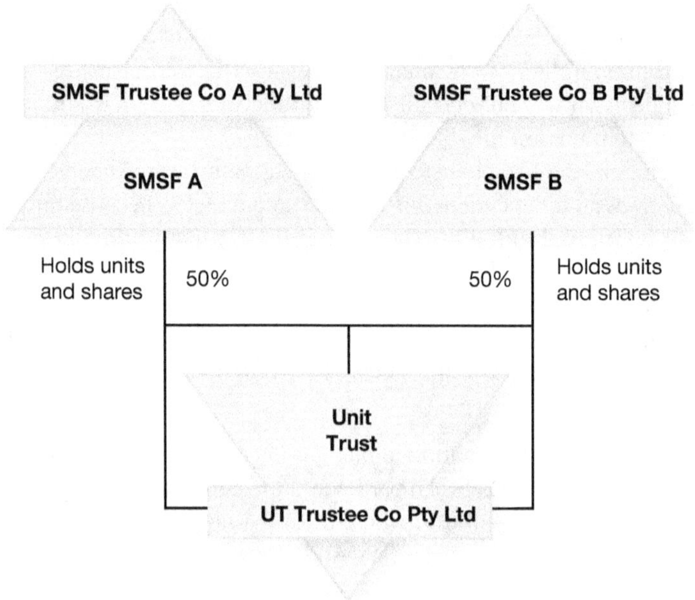

IHAs

An SMSF may invest in a unit trust (subject to the application of the non-arm's length income provisions discussed below) provided that the unit trust is not a related party of the fund.

As noted earlier, there is a prohibition in the SIS Act which restricts the amount of IHAs that can be owned or invested by an SMSF to generally 5% of the market value of an SMSFs assets.

A unit trust that is controlled by a related party of an SMSF will be an IHA and caught by this prohibition, unless the trust satisfies the exemption in regulation 13.22C of the SIS Regulations (i.e. it is an ungeared unit trust).

With certain exclusions, an IHA of an SMSF is an asset that is any one of the following:

- a a loan to, or an investment in, a related party of the fund;
- b an investment in a related trust of the fund; or
- c an asset of the fund that is subject to a lease or lease arrangement between the trustee of the fund and a related party of the fund.

Generally, an SMSF cannot lend to, or invest in, a related party or related trust of the fund, where the loans, or the values of the assets that are the subject of the investment or lease arrangement, are greater than 5% of the market value of the fund's total assets.

If an SMSF has IHA with a value of more than 5% of the market value of the fund's total assets, then:

- a the trustee may be disqualified;
- b the fund may be made non-complying;
- c a range of other penalties may be imposed (including prohibitions on acquiring further IHAs and prosecution).

Ungeared unit trusts

The test for whether a trust is controlled by a related party of an SMSF requires consideration of the fixed entitlements of the unitholders. In particular, a related party of an SMSF will be deemed to control the trust if the fund or its associates have a fixed entitlement to more than 50% of the capital or income of the trust.

There is an exception to the IHA test in SIS Regulation 13.22C for a unit trust that does not have any borrowings, notwithstanding that the trust may be a related party of an SMSF.

This commonly arises where an SMSF wishes to make an investment through a unit trust with other (non-superannuation fund) unitholders who can borrow to invest in the trust, or if no borrowing is required to fund the investment.

To be eligible for the exemption, the following conditions need to be met:

- a the trust does not borrow;
- b the trust does not invest in or loan money to individuals or other entities (other than deposits with authorised deposit-taking institutions);
- c there is no charge over an asset of the trust;
- d the trust has not acquired an asset from a related party of the fund other than business real property;
- e the trust has not acquired an asset (apart from business real property) that had been owned by a related party of the fund in the previous three years;

f the trust does not directly or indirectly lease assets to related parties other than business real property;
g the trust does not conduct a business; and
h the trust conducts all transactions on an arm's length basis.

Prior to 12 August 1999, an investment by a superannuation fund in a related unit trust was not an IHA. The transitional arrangements following the expansion of the definition of an IHA permit a fund to maintain an investment in a pre-12 August 1999 unit trust where the investment was not previously an IHA.

However, it is relevant to also bear in mind that the sole purpose test and the non-arm's length income provisions may still apply to the investment. Following 30 June 2009, any further investments in a pre-1999 unit trust will be an IHA unless a specific exemption applies.

Non-arm's length income

Income derived by an SMSF as a beneficiary of a trust, other than because of holding a fixed entitlement to the income, is non-arm's length income of the entity and will be taxed at penalty rates under the non-arm's length income provisions of the Tax Act. It is therefore important to ensure that the unit trust is a fixed trust for taxation purposes if the unitholder is an SMSF.

Income derived by a superannuation fund as a beneficiary of a fixed trust will also be non-arm's length income if:

a the fund acquired the entitlement under a scheme, or the income was derived under a scheme, the parties to which were not dealing with each other at arm's length; and
b the amount of the income is more than the amount that the fund might have been expected to derive if those parties had been dealing at arm's length.

To avoid the impact of the non-arm's length income rules, it is therefore vital for SMSFs to ensure that:

a no distributions are made to an SMSF from a discretionary trust; and
b where an SMSF owns units in a unit trust, that the unit trust is a fixed trust for tax purposes.

The ATO has expressed the view that the meaning of a 'fixed trust' must be ascertained from the terms of the relevant trust deed.

It is also relevant to note that the non-arm's length income rules may apply where an SMSF allows its fixed entitlement to remain as an unpaid present entitlement, as this generally does not reflect an arm's length arrangement.

When allowing unpaid present trust entitlements in favour of an SMSF, it is therefore necessary to ensure that interest on those unpaid distributions is paid by the trust at market rates as would be the case if the SMSF and trust were dealing with each other at arm's length.

Whether a unit trust is in fact a fixed trust is an area that has been the subject of significant uncertainty.

In 2016, the ATO did release Practice Compliance Guidelines concerning its view of what is a fixed trust. Unfortunately, the release by the ATO is problematic for SMSFs for at least four reasons, namely:

a it only considered the meaning of 'fixed trust' for the purpose of the trust loss provisions under the Tax Act;
b the drafting approach of the ATO is non-definitive; in other words the ATO confirms it will retain the discretion to deem a trust not to be fixed despite what it sets out in the guidelines;
c a number of issues that most specialists would believe to be critical, were not considered in the guidelines;
d furthermore, the guidelines are not themselves binding on the ATO.

Subject to the above comments, broadly it seems to be accepted that the following factors will be relevant to supporting that a trust is a fixed trust:

a the trustee cannot create different rights or different classes of units;
b all units on issue must have the same rights to receive income and capital of the trust;
c units must be allotted for market value;
d all income and capital of the trust must be distributed in proportion to the unitholdings, i.e. there is no discretion held by the trustee;
e partly paid units cannot be issued;
f the trust deed requires all unitholders to agree on the redemption of units and any redemption must be at market value;
g all valuations of the trust fund, and in turn the determination of unit values, must be conducted by a valuer in accordance with 'applicable Australian accounting principles';
h the trustee cannot make gifts; and
i the unanimous consent of all unitholders is required to vary the trust deed and the variation power should prohibit amendments to any of the above provisions.

Anti-avoidance rules

Finally in relation to investment structures for SMSFs, it is important to note that when taxation issues are considered as part of deciding how best to implement a specific transaction or wider arrangement, there is a risk that the ATO might review the transaction or arrangement and apply the general anti-avoidance rules contained in part IVA of the Tax Act.

Very broadly, part IVA may apply to the superannuation arrangements summarised above where it can be objectively determined from all the circumstances that the dominant purpose of any party to the transaction or arrangement, or to a part of the transaction or arrangement (Scheme), is to obtain a tax benefit for that party or another party associated with the Scheme.

The ATO must make a specific determination that part IVA applies. The ATO can then cancel the tax benefits otherwise obtained, reconstruct the transaction or arrangement for tax purposes and issue assessments, including penalties and interest relating to the disallowed tax benefit.

The interpretation of part IVA is highly technical and its application in each case requires a detailed consideration of the current case law and all the relevant facts. Furthermore, unless a binding ruling under part IVA is obtained from the ATO, it is not possible to provide certainty about its possible application.

Template Investment Strategy

User Note: All aspects of this document needs to be reviewed and amended to reflect the circumstances of the Fund. Particular attention is needed in relation to items marked '#'. This document is a template only and specialist advice should be obtained before it is relied on.

1 Overview

Fund Profile

1.1 The [#insert] Superannuation Fund (Fund) is an allocated accumulation fund established on to provide lump sum retirement benefits for members as well as death/disablement protection for members and the dependants of members. Membership of the Fund is voluntary, and upon joining, members are required to provide certain minimum information to the Trustees.

1.2 The Fund has members who are aged [#insert] respectively at the time of this document.

1.3 The personal assets of the members are as follows: [#insert list of assets, approximate value and any debt].

1.4 It is not intended that other members will be admitted to the fund. The current intention is for the members to receive a retirement benefit at the following ages: [#insert].

Benefits

1.5 The current intention is to pay [# lump sum, or pension] benefits upon retirement of the members. The Trustee shall invest Fund assets having regard to the need to realise the investments at the members' dates of retirement (or such later date as the member nominates in accordance with the rules governing the payment of benefits from complying superannuation funds).

1.6 There are no unallocated reserves in the fund and it is not intended to maintain any reserves.

Trustee Details

1.7 The Trustee of the Fund is [# insert] (Trustee) which company has 2 directors being the members.

2 Future Contributions

2.1 The members of the Fund will have sufficient death and disability cover provided through life cover in the Fund to enable the Trustees to take a long term perspective in setting the investment objectives of the Fund.

3 Past Investment Performance/Asset Mix

3.1 The past investment performance of the Fund has exceeded the CPI by [# insert]% over the last five years.

3.2 The assets of the fund are currently invested in the following proportions [# insert]:

(a) Public Company Shares

(b) Fixed Interest

(c) In-house Asset

4 Investment Objectives

General Objectives

4.1 The Trustee will at all times act prudently to pursue the maximum rate of return possible, subject to acceptable risk parameters, and the maintenance of appropriate diversification.

4.2 The Trustee will ensure that all investments are authorised under the trust deed, are made for the sole purpose of providing benefits to members and the dependants of members, and are made in accordance with the legislative requirements applicable to complying superannuation funds.

4.3 The Trustee will invest to ensure sufficient liquidity is retained within the Fund to meet benefit payments due, and will adjust its specific objectives where it believes the risk profile of the Fund has changed.

4.4 The Trustee will make investments in conjunction with members or any related parties only, the Principal Employer or on an arm's length basis, and in accordance with the in-house asset limits or any other legislative requirements.

Specific Objectives

4.5 Having considered the liability profile of the Fund, the Trustee has adopted the following objectives for the investment of the assets of the Fund:

(a) to achieve an investment return (net of tax and charges) that exceeds CPI by at least 4% per annum when measured over a rolling 10 year period;

(b) to achieve an investment return (net of tax and charges) that exceeds cash rates by at least 2% per annum when measured over a rolling 5 year period;

(c) to have a low expectation of negative returns in any 12 month period;

(d) to limit exposure to equities and property investment to under 70% of the assets of the Fund in order to limit earnings volatility; and

(e) to ensure the Fund generates sufficient cash flow to discharge administration expenses and other outgoings.

4.6 The Trustee will consider the implementation of these objectives through a single asset strategy where it considers that appropriate.

Review

4.7 The investment objectives of the Fund will be reviewed annually and at such other times as a significant event occurs which affects the Fund.

5 Investment Strategy

5.1 In order to achieve the investment objectives of the Fund, the Trustee wishes to adopt and pursue the strategy set out hereunder. The Trustee reserves the right to implement more than one strategy as it sees fit, and to offer separate strategies to members. The Trustee also reserves the right to implement separate and different action plans in the acquisition and disposal of assets pursuant to this strategy.

Diversification

5.2 The Trustee intends to achieve a level of diversification along the following parameters [#insert]:

Asset class	Range	Actual as at
Property (a) Unit trust and (b) direct	%	%

Equities Public company shares	%	%
Cash Cash management (a) Australian (b) International	%	%
Other assets (eg options, futures, art, collectibles etc)	%	%
TOTAL		

5.3 In considering the degree of diversification appropriate to the Fund, the Trustee has determined to take into account the following:

(a) the existing assets of the Fund;

(b) the existing personal assets of the members;

(c) its access to expert investment advice;

(d) the existing and projected membership and assets of the Fund; and

(e) the decision not to implement a reserving policy.

Fund Demographics

5.4 The Trustee has implemented its strategy taking into account the age of the members and their likely dates of retirement. It has also taken into account the expressed intention of the members to receive their benefits as [#insert—lump sums/allocated pensions] upon retirement.

Costs of investing

5.5 The Trustee will seek to minimise the investment costs it incurs, however at times upfront investment costs will be payable in order to obtain the best investment products that align with the Fund's overall investment strategy. The Trustee acknowledges that costs and penalties may also be part of the cost of implementing this investment strategy.

Performance Monitoring

5.6 To monitor the success of the investment policy in achieving the investment objectives, the Trustee will take the following steps:

(a) compare investment returns against investment objectives on an annual basis;

(b) compare the investment performance of the Fund against a sample group of superannuation master funds;

(c) compare investment returns against cash rates available over a 12 month period and will review this strategy on an annual basis or on such other basis as it believes appropriate.

Benchmarks

5.7 The Trustee will also measure the success of this investment strategy against certain benchmarks and indices. The nominated benchmarks for performance are:

(a) Australian shares—all ordinaries accumulation index;

(b) Liquid assets—average cash management trusts;

(c) Australian fixed trusts—commonwealth all series all maturities and accumulation index;

(d) Property trusts—average of composite property accumulation index; and

(e) In-house asset loans—average rates for comparable loans from major banks and legislative interest requirements.

Borrowing

5.8 The Trustee may, where consistent with the Fund's overall investment strategy, enter into limited recourse borrowing arrangements. Any decision by the Trustee to borrow funds must take the following factors into account:

(a) The risk involved in borrowing funds and holding an asset under a limited recourse borrowing arrangement;

(b) The likely return from the arrangement;

(c) The liquidity and cash flow consequences of entering into the arrangement;

(d) The time the members have until they retire;

(e) The impact of the arrangement on the Fund's cash flow requirements; and

(f) The investment risk tolerance of the members.

6 Asset Management Strategy

6.1 The Trustee will have regard to the following principles in the implementation of its investment strategy and the actual making of its investments.

6.2 The Trustee will specifically consider whether the unit trust it is intending to invest in is a fixed trust for tax purposes.

Unit Trusts

6.3 Prior to acquiring or disposing of any units in an unlisted unit trust the Trustee will obtain and consider property and rental valuations of all assets held by the unit trust to satisfy itself that the price of the units reflect true market values and constitutes a prudent investment/ disposal on an arm's length basis.

6.4 The Trustee will also ascertain the intentions of the trustee of the unit trust in relation to borrowing (if any) and the use of the property as security.

Direct Property

6.5 Prior to acquiring or disposing of any property to be held directly by the Fund, the Trustee will obtain and consider property and rental valuations to satisfy itself that the price of the property reflects true market value and constitutes a prudent investment/disposal on an arm's length basis.

6.6 In obtaining a tenant (if any) for any property held by the Fund, the Trustee may enter into an associate, provided that a written lease agreement is made and the transaction is entered into on an arm's length basis with regular rental reviews.

6.7 In determining the proportion of Fund assets to be invested directly in property, the Trustee shall take into account the liability profile, diversification and liquidity requirements of the Fund.

Shares (Non-Associated Proprietary Companies)

6.8 Prior to acquiring (or disposing) of any shares in non-associated proprietary companies, the Trustee shall obtain a valuation to satisfy itself that the price of the shares reflect true market values and constitute a prudent investment/disposal.

6.9 The Trustee shall also take into account the saleability, security and dividend return of the shares and will ensure that the acquisition is not an in-house asset beyond acceptable limits or otherwise prohibited by legislation.

Shares (Public Company)

6.10 Prior to acquiring (or disposing) of any shares in public companies, the Trustee shall consider the portfolio profile of the Fund and the diversification of shareholding across different market sectors (industrial, retail, mining, agri business, financial, banking, etc.) with a view to attempting to obtain appropriate diversification.

6.11 The Trustee will also take into account any advice received in relation to expected capital growth and dividend income.

Debentures/First Mortgage

6.12 Prior to investing in any debenture/first mortgage the Trustee shall consider the period of investment, the security offered, the accessibility of funds, the return and likely interest rate movements.

Cash Management

6.13 Prior to investing or realising any cash management funds the Trustee shall consider the rate of return and security of such investment against the expected rate of return offered by alternative investments to cash (including, for example, fixed interest and bonds).

Artwork/Antiques/Collectibles

6.14 Prior to acquiring any collectibles as an investment of the Fund the Trustee will obtain an independent professional valuation from a qualified valuer and will ensure the asset represents a minor part of Fund assets. It will investigate future saleability of the asset and the likely price movements in future.

6.15 Prior to leasing any collectibles held by the Fund to any party the Trustee shall determine the commercial rental rate having regard to advice which the Trustee obtains from a qualified source. Any lease is only to be entered into under a written lease agreement made on an arm's length basis with obligations set out for full maintenance and insurance.

6.16 Prior to disposing of any collectibles held by the Fund, the Trustee will obtain an independent professional valuation from a qualified valuer. The Trustee must also determine whether the proposed timing of the disposal is in the best interest of members having regard to the fluctuations in the value of the type of collectible of which the Trustee wishes to dispose.

In-House Assets

6.17 The Trustee will only acquire in-house assets if permitted under legislation governing complying superannuation funds and if the Trustee determines that it is in the best interest of members.

Financial Derivatives

6.18 The Trustee will develop a separate specific investment strategy if any form of financial derivative is to be acquired by the Fund, including:

- (a) options;
- (b) futures;
- (c) foreign currency;
- (d) swaps;
- (e) crowd source lending;
- (f) contracts for the difference (CFDs);
- (g) structured or synthetic bonds or shares.

7 Insurance

7.1 The Trustee will regularly consider whether the Fund should hold insurance cover for its members and based on an analysis of the needs of the members, cash flow requirements for the Fund and the insurance already held by the members outside of the Fund, the following insurance was considered appropriate for the Trustee to obtain [# insert]:

Member	Insurance type	Amount

The above investment strategy has been prepared with reference to the checklist set out in the Schedule to this document is confirmed by the Trustee on [#insert].

[# insert signing provisions for Trustee]

Fund Investments Involving Associated Persons and Entities

1 SIS Requirements

Prohibition Against Acquisition of Assets from Related Parties

1.1 Is the asset to be acquired from a 'related party' (as defined under SIS) of the Fund?

1.2 Is the asset which is being acquired business real property of a related party of a member?

1.3 If yes, all of the following requirements must be satisfied:

   (a) the asset must be acquired at market value;

   (b) after the acquisition of the property all property acquired from the related party may be up to 100% of the total value of the assets of the Fund; and

   (c) the acquisition must be a freehold or leasehold interest in real property used wholly or exclusively in a business.

1.4 Is the asset which is being acquired a listed security?

1.5 If yes, it must be acquired at market value.

1.6 Transactions involving use of interposed entities. These should be vetted by professional advisers to ensure that they are not caught by the anti-avoidance provisions of SIS.

Arm's Length Basis Requirement

1.7 Is the transaction being entered into on an arm's length basis?

1.8 This requirement is satisfied if the terms of the transaction taken as a whole are no more or less favourable to either party than would be the case if it involved arm's length parties.

In-house Asset Rules

1.9 Does the investment involve a loan to or an investment in a related parry or related trust of the Fund or an asset of the Fund subject to a lease or lease arrangement between the Fund and a related party? If so, the level of such investments should not exceed 5% of the market value of the Fund.

1.10 Prepare action plan to monitor level of such investments to ensure that the level is regularly monitored, in line with Part 8 of SIS.

1.11 Unit trust and other complex structures or transactions should be vetted by professional advisers for possible breaches of the in-house asset rules.

Loans and Financial Assistance to Members and their Relatives

1.12 Does the investment involve a loan to a member, relative or associate of a member? If so, such an investment is not permitted.

1.13 Consider whether the investment involves giving financial assistance to the member, relative or associate of a member. If so, such an investment should not be made.

2 Prudential Requirements

2.1 The Trustee should obtain an independent valuation of the asset from a qualified person.

2.2 If the non-arm's length person from whom the asset is to be acquired is a trustee or a director of the trustee company, full disclosure should be made to the co-trustees/co-directors, of the nature of the individual's interest in the asset. If possible, the person should not take part in the Trustee's deliberations regarding the acquisition of the asset.

2.3 The acquisition of the asset must conform with the current investment objectives and strategy of the Fund.

2.4 The transaction should be thoroughly documented and minuted and deposits/purchase moneys must be paid.

2.5 In determining the market price of any shares to be acquired the Trustee should take into account whether the purchase is "ex dividend" or "cum dividend". Similarly with unit trust acquisitions, the purchase price should reflect any income distribution available.

Appointment of Fund Investment Manager Questions To Be Used In The Selection Criteria Of An Investment Manager

1 Organisational Issues

1.1 What is ownership structure of investment manager?

1.2 What is the management structure?

1.3 Does the investment manager have an office in the same city as Trustee? If not, how will it service the Fund?

1.4 What are the business objectives of the investment manager?
1.5 How long has the company been in business in Australia?
1.6 Are there any potential conflicts of interest? If so how are these dealt with?
1.7 What other affiliated services can the investment manager provide (custodial, brokerage etc.).
1.8 Does the investment manager have adequate professional indemnity insurance cover?

2 Resources

2.1 Who are the people to be involved in the provision of investment advisory services?
2.2 What role will these people be playing with the Fund?
2.3 What data base and other analysis facilities does the investment manager have and what will be available for the Fund?
2.4 What types of research does the investment manager carry out and how does it go about it?

3 Fees

3.1 On what basis are fees charged?
3.2 What is the breakup of fees on entry, management, and exit?
3.3 How often are fees reviewed and what advice is provided on review?

Chapter 3

ESTATE PLANNING AND ASSET PROTECTION

Overview

Superannuation is often an individual's single most significant asset upon their retirements and potentially at the time of death.

The policies of several successive federal governments to encourage wealth accumulation via superannuation have resulted in a boom in retirement savings.

Despite the increase in wealth being held in superannuation, the estate planning steps necessary to ensure that an individual's entitlements pass as intended upon their death are commonly misunderstood.

The impact of these misunderstandings can be exacerbated when insurance is held in the superannuation environment, increasing the value of the wealth needing to ultimately pass to a beneficiary.

It is therefore important to have a comprehensive estate plan in place which addresses both estate and non-estate assets, particularly for SMSFs.

Proper planning can also reduce the likelihood that, after death, the recipients of superannuation benefits (and other assets) will have to pay unnecessary tax or find those assets exposed to unexpected risks.

The role of the trustee

In administering an SMSF, a trustee is normally given a number of discretionary powers.

It is generally up to the trustee to determine whether a person's superannuation benefits are paid to a dependant directly or to their estate. If a trustee pays superannuation death benefits directly to a person's dependants, then the estate is bypassed.

If however superannuation benefits are distributed to the estate of the former member then they will be dealt with by the member's will (or the intestacy rules if there is no valid will).

Benefits paid via an estate can in turn be distributed to, for example, a testamentary trust set up under the former member's will. Testamentary trusts are outside the scope of this book, however the author has published a book titled 'The Seven Key Aspects of Testamentary Trusts'.

The trustee of an SMSF may also have the discretion to determine the form the death benefits are paid—that is either as a lump sum or income stream, or possibly a combination of both. Importantly however, if a benefit is to be paid from an SMSF to an estate it can only be paid in the form of a lump sum.

Broadly, the exercise of discretion by a trustee of SMSF, for example, when determining how to pay a death benefit where a non-BDBN has been made is not subject to review by the court unless one of the following three factors is present:

a The trustee does not act in good faith;
b The trustee does not give real and genuine consideration to the exercise of the discretion and the purposes for which the discretion was granted; or

c Reasons for the decision are provided by the trustee, but those reasons are unsound.

Trusteeship issues within an SMSF

The trusteeship of an SMSF is governed by section 17A of the SIS Act.

The trustee may be either:

a a company operating as a corporate trustee, with each member of the SMSF being a director of the company; or
b more than one individual trustee, again with each member being a trustee.

An additional consideration when appointing trustees is that generally a person who is not a member of the SMSF is not permitted to be a trustee (or director of a corporate trustee). Single member funds are an exception to this rule as an SMSF is not permitted to have a sole individual trustee.

Consequently, a single member fund can appoint a second trustee.

Similarly, single member SMSFs can have a corporate trustee with two directors, with the second director being someone other than the member (although a single member fund can also have a company with the member as sole director).

The rules in relation to trusteeship obviously significantly impact on the control of an SMSF following the incapacity or death of a member.

Incapacity

Special rules apply where a member of an SMSF is incapacitated, in which case their legal personal representative (typically their attorney, pursuant to an enduring power of attorney) is permitted to act in that member's place as a trustee or director.

However the SIS Act merely authorises the appointment from a superannuation compliance perspective and does not set out the legal process by which the appointment can occur.

An analysis is therefore required of the relevant instrument (the trust deed or company constitution) and legislation (the Trusts Acts in each state or the Corporations Act).

If the SMSF has a corporate trustee, the attorney will usually need to rely on either:

a a resolution by the other directors appointing them as a director, pursuant to a rule in the company's constitution; or
b a resolution by the shareholders appointing them as a director, pursuant to the Corporations Act.

This process can obviously raise a number of issues where the incapacitated individual was the sole director or a majority shareholder of the company.

Similarly, if the SMSF has individual trustees, the attorney will usually be reliant on the remaining co-trustees passing a resolution pursuant to the deed to make the appointment.

Practically, the only way in which an attorney under an enduring power of attorney could act in the role as trustee for an SMSF would be for the existing member to be removed from their role as trustee or director of the corporate trustee, and for the attorney under that member's enduring power of attorney to be appointed as the new trustee or director in place of the member.

Importantly, the person seeking to become a trustee or director needs to be appointed under an enduring power of attorney of the member who is seeking to be replaced. A general power of attorney will not be sufficient.

If, in time, a member no longer requires the attorney to be the trustee/director, the attorney would resign as trustee/director and the member would be re-appointed as trustee/director.

Alternatively, if the SMSF trustee:

a is an individual, the SMSF trust deed should provide the members with the power to remove and appoint a trustee either personally or through a 'principal' style role (if applicable). If the power to remove and appoint is left with the trustee for the time being (that is, the attorney) that may cause the members difficulty if the attorney refuses to resign; or
b is a company, the constitution for the SMSF trustee should ideally give any fund members who are shareholders power to remove and appoint a director of the company.

Death

Upon the death of a member, steps must be taken to ensure the trusteeship of the SMSF continues to comply with the requirements above.

Individual trustees

As a starting point assets of an SMSF must be held in the trustee's name.

With individual trustees, this will require the transferring of the titles to all assets to the new trustee when a new member is admitted to an SMSF and in turn removing a trustee's name when a member leaves a fund upon death, retirement due to incapacity or otherwise.

This administrative burden can be time-consuming and costly.

The nomination of successor trustees is important when an SMSF has individuals as trustees. Some SMSFs have a 'founder' or 'principal' role vested in someone other than the members. This can be a powerful role as such a person will generally have the power to appoint or remove a trustee or vary the trust deed.

Without such a role, any remaining trustee/s, or if there are no trustees remaining, the LPR of the last remaining trustee has the power to appoint the new trustee.

Corporate trustees

When members are admitted to, or cease membership of an SMSF with a corporate trustee all that is required is that the person becomes, or ceases to be, a director of the company.

A notification of this change must be sent to the ASIC within 14 days of the change, although generally of time will be provided where a failure to comply with the 14 day period is due to the death of the director.

As the legal title to all the assets remains vested in the company (which continues to act as trustee), a corporate trustee of an SMSF can save considerable time and effort.

The main disadvantages of having a corporate trustee of an SMSF are the:

a upfront cost of establishing the trustee company;
b extra documentation required when establishing the SMSF; and
c ongoing annual fee payable to ASIC, although where the company is a 'special purpose' company and has as its sole activity acting as trustee of an SMSF, a discounted annual fee of around 25% of the normal annual fee is payable to ASIC.

Conversely, the main advantage of appointing individual trustees is that it is quick, simple and initially inexpensive. There are no establishment costs, less ongoing fees and less initial paper work required when setting up the SMSF.

For completeness it is noted that a corporate trustee of a borrowing trust does not satisfy the definition of 'special purpose company', despite the fact that an SMSF will be the sole beneficiary and the trust is therefore essentially part of the superannuation structure.

This is because a special purpose company only includes:

> *'a company..... if the sole purpose of the company is to act as the trustee of a regulated superannuation fund within the meaning of the SIS Act.'*

If the deceased member is a shareholder in the corporate trustee of an SMSF, it is important to specify the recipient of those shares in their will.

The Corporations Act gives shareholders voting rights and allows them to vote out directors of the company (subject to any provision to the contrary in the constitution of the corporate trustee).

Shareholders thus hold a considerable amount of power and care must be taken to ensure that appropriate beneficiaries of the shares are chosen and included in the will.

The beneficiaries holding the shares will often have the responsibility of appointing a new director of the trustee company of the SMSF.

The new director would, in turn, along with any other directors of the company, exercise discretion in paying death benefits, unless a valid BDBN has been made.

The powers of a person who receives the shares in the corporate trustee of an SMSF are subject to at least two possible limitations, namely:

a any 'founder' or 'principal' role under the SMSF trust deed vested in someone other than the shareholders of the trustee company (as mentioned above); or
b prohibitions set out in the constitution of the trustee company around the rights attaching to the shares. For example, the shares of a member may be automatically redeemed on the death of the member, or the voting rights attaching to the shares may be limited to a percentage equal to the proportionate share of the relevant members' member balance in the SMSF.

Income stream overview

A superannuation death benefit may only be paid as an income stream to a 'dependant' of the deceased member.

As noted above, there is a $1.6M (subject to indexation for inflation) transfer cap for each member of an SMSF. This means a surviving spouse who receives a reversionary pension from their partner (or commence a pension post death), has this value included when calculating their remaining transfer cap.

If an income stream superannuation death benefit is paid to a child, then the income stream must be converted to a lump sum superannuation death benefit once the child reaches the age of 25, unless the child is disabled. The decision to pay an income stream to a child needs to take this into account, especially if there is likely to be a large lump sum passing to the child at age 25.

Importantly, each child receives their own $1.6M transfer cap linked to the deceased parent's cap. This means that not only does the child receive their own $1.6M (subject to indexation for inflation) transfer cap on retirement they also have access to each parent's transfer cap. In other words, on the death of two parents, the transfer cap for the child could be entitled to a proportionate share of a cap of up to $3.2 million.

Where a member has reached preservation age, and is already receiving their superannuation benefit as an income stream prior to death, it is possible to nominate a reversionary beneficiary for their benefit to ensure that, upon the member's death, the income stream is paid to their nominated beneficiary.

The tax treatment of both lump sum and income stream superannuation death benefits depends upon a number of factors and specific advice should always be obtained with reference to the exact factual matrix and current laws.

Ultimately, the trust deed governing a superannuation fund (together with any valid nominations) will determine the process for dealing with a person's superannuation assets upon their death.

Estate Planning Costs Paid Through an SMSF

In order to obtain the concessional taxation available for superannuation savings, an SMSF must have its sole purpose as being the provision of benefits to members on retirement, or their dependants or LPR on death.

In this context, one issue that is often raised is whether an SMSF can pay the costs of ensuring its members have their estate planning affairs in order.

In the absence of any specific guidance from the ATO in this area, there are a range of views about the legitimacy of this approach.

Some advisers believe that any estate planning related expense is clearly incurred in order to help provide for the dependants or LPR of a member and therefore properly payable by an SMSF.

The conservative position is that either all estate planning costs should be incurred by members personally, or alternatively where they may be paid by the SMSF, there must be a direct and clear nexus between the expense incurred and the ultimate provision of benefits to dependants or LPR on the death of a member.

While the conservative approach seems to be that all estate planning costs should be incurred by members personally, practically, there are a number of examples where having an SMSF incur the relevant expense would appear reasonably arguable, including:

a where an SMSF trust deed is being updated as part of an estate planning exercise, clearly these costs should be incurred by the fund;

b where, as part of the update, BDBNs are prepared (either on a standalone basis or 'hardwired' into the trust deed of the SMSF), then again these costs are legitimately payable by the fund;

c where superannuation makes up a significant component of a member's overall wealth and the member intends (either via binding or non-BDBNs) for their superannuation entitlements to pass via their will, then the costs of the will (including any testamentary trusts incorporated into the documentation) should also be able to be paid by the SMSF;

d strategic advice to members in relation to the impact of death on their superannuation entitlements should also be properly payable by the SMSF; and

e while the nexus might be slightly less obvious, ensuring that a member has a legal personal representative able to take over the trusteeship of an SMSF may also justify a fund incurring costs for implementing a member's enduring power of attorney.

As with many similar topics, the general position outlined above will depend on the particular factual situation.

For completeness it is noted that part of the confusion with the rules in this area, particularly for financial advisers and risk advisers, undoubtedly is because of the relatively vague standards that most licensees seem to impose.

Some licensee rules provided that advisers can charge an SMSF for all advice that was either product related or strategically relevant to the SMSF.

In turn, often the rules will state that charging the SMSF for any other advice that is not so 'related' will potentially breach the sole purpose test and is therefore prohibited.

Unfortunately, the vagueness of the rules under this type of approach can make it difficult for advisers and clients alike to make decisions in relation to areas such as binding death benefit nominations and wider estate planning documentation, and until there is clearer guidance from, for example, the ATO, there is likely to be continuing uncertainty.

Deductibility of SMSF expenses

As a general rule, deductibility of expenditure incurred by an SMSF is determined under section8-1 of the Tax Act, unless:

- a a specific deduction provision in the Tax Act applies; or
- b a provision of the Tax Act makes the expenditure specifically non-deductible.

To be deductible under section8-1, the expenditure must not be a loss or outgoing of capital, or of a capital nature, or of a private or domestic nature.

Broadly, the following types of expenses typically incurred by an SMSF are deductible under section8-1:

- a costs of complying with the SIS Act, unless the cost is a capital expense;
- b costs in connection with the calculation and payment of benefits to members;
- c investment adviser fees and costs in providing pre-retirement services to members;
- d other administration costs incurred in managing the SMSF;
- e costs for advice where provided by a qualified lawyer.

Refreshing of cost base

Historically, after death, in addition to any taxes triggered on the payment of funds or distribution of assets to dependants, an SMSF itself was required to pay tax, at a rate of 10%, on the difference between the cost base and market value of each asset the subject of payment at the date of death.

This lead to approach whereby there was a focus on the fact that any sale of a capital asset prior to death (assuming the SMSF was in pension mode) was tax-free.

In these circumstances, one strategy often adopted was to actively 'refresh' the cost base of the assets in the SMSF. This was achieved by the following steps:

- a assets with large capital gains are regularly sold and then reacquired, or other assets are acquired;
- b the sale and reacquisition ensure that the cost base of the asset, for the SMSF, is regularly uplifted; and
- c on death, the likely capital gain in relation to any particular asset is therefore minimised.

This approach needed to be managed carefully to ensure the anti-avoidance provisions of the Tax Act are not enlivened.

Due to industry feedback, the rules were changed to provide the tax exemption for pension earnings continued from the date of death until the date of distribution of the death benefit to the member.

With the $1.6M transfer balance cap regime there may be situations where this style of strategy becomes important in the future.

Accessing disablement proceeds via superannuation

Best practice often dictates that SMSF members should obtain insurance protection on the basis of an inability to work in their 'own', as opposed to 'any' occupation.

The satisfaction of the 'own' occupation test is obviously easier than the condition of release set out under the superannuation legislation, being that a member must be incapable of working in 'any' occupation.

Where insurance is owned via a superannuation fund there is therefore a risk that while the fund will receive an insurance payout, it will be unable to release it to the member until some other condition of release is satisfied (for example, reaching the retirement age).

Historically therefore, the conservative view was undoubtedly that own occupation insurance should always be owned outside super. Importantly, since 1 July 2014, own occupation insurance is no longer available via superannuation, subject to a grandfathering for arrangements already in place before that date.

For those pre-existing arrangements, there appears to be a pragmatic approach adopted, particularly by those with policies via an SMSF. This approach involves assuming that a trustee (who will also be a member of the relevant fund) will adopt a liberal interpretation of the 'any' occupation definition under the superannuation legislation and therefore always allow the release of insurance proceeds.

SMSFs and asset protection

Movement into bankruptcy

A lot must happen before a trustee in bankruptcy becomes involved.

In particular, there must be a debt.

If that debt is a judgment debt, there will have been a claim that has been successfully prosecuted in the courts.

There must then have been a failure to meet that debt.

The creditor must then have sought to appoint a trustee in bankruptcy to the debtor's estate.

Depending on the circumstances, other arrangements might be considered in order to avoid the appointment of a trustee in bankruptcy. The debtor might consider entering into an informal agreement with creditors, or entering into arrangements under parts IX or X of the Bankruptcy Act.

A discussion of these various arrangements and options is outside the scope of this book.

'Claw back' rules

In considering claims that might be brought by a trustee in bankruptcy, it is relevant to bear in mind the voidable transaction provisions in the Bankruptcy Act. These provisions, often referred to as 'claw back' provisions, enable the trustee in bankruptcy to trace and reclaim assets that were transferred prior to a person becoming bankrupt.

In particular, a transfer can be overturned, subject to certain exclusions:

- a if the transfer took place within four years before the commencement of the bankruptcy where no consideration was paid or where consideration was less than market value; or
- b if the transfer at any time before the commencement of the bankruptcy and at the time of the transfer the person was insolvent, where no consideration was paid or where consideration was less than market value; or
- c if the transfer took place within six months before the commencement of the bankruptcy, the transfer is to a creditor, the creditor obtains a preference, priority or advantage over other creditors and at the time of the transfer the transferor was insolvent; or
- d at any time where the main purpose in making the transfer is to prevent the transferred property from becoming divisible, or to hinder or to delay the process of making property available for division, among creditors.

It should be remembered that, as the commencement of the bankruptcy may be dated from the first act of bankruptcy within the six months before a relevant petition was presented, up to a further six months could be added to these periods of 'claw back'.

Companies and trusts

Similar provisions to those found in the Bankruptcy Act regarding voidable preferences are in the Corporations Act. Under section588FE of the Bankruptcy Act the following transactions are voidable:

- a an insolvent transaction within six months of the commencement of winding up of the company;
- b an insolvent and uncommercial transaction within two years of the commencement of winding up;
- c an insolvent transaction with a related party entered into within four years of the commencement of winding up; and
- d an insolvent transaction which the company entered into for the purpose of defeating or delaying creditors—within ten years of the commencement of winding up.

The same rules apply to trusts depending whether the trustee is an individual or company.

Superannuation and bankruptcy

Legislative provisions

Historically the Bankruptcy Act provided that all property that belonged to a bankrupt at the start of a bankruptcy was divisible amongst the creditors of the bankrupt. Property was defined to exclude interest in a superannuation fund if certain qualifications were met. This meant that this protection of superannuation was not absolute.

From 1 July 2007 however assets held via a superannuation fund can only be 'clawed back' if the main purpose of the transferor was either to:

- a prevent the transferred property being available to creditors; or
- b hinder or delay the process of making property available for division among creditors.

To determine the main purpose for making the contribution it is presumed to be an attempt to defeat creditors if it can reasonably be inferred from all the circumstances that at the time of the transfer the transferor was, or was about to become, insolvent.

If insolvency is not an issue at the time of transfer, both sections provide that when determining the transferor's main purpose for making the transfer, regard must be had to whether the transferor had established any pattern of making contributions to one or more superannuation funds and if so whether the transfer under examination is out of character.

Therefore, as an example, contributions are unlikely to be made with the intention of defeating creditors if contributions have been made every year for the past 5-10 years.

However, it is debateable (as another example) if a contribution will be sufficiently 'unusual' to be for the purpose of defeating creditors if a person makes contributions utilising the accelerated non-concessional regime, profiled elsewhere in this book. This is despite the fact that such contributions are at law only able to be made in sporadic instalments.

Payments from superannuation

Generally lump sum payments from an SMSF to a bankrupt are protected from a trustee in bankruptcy, including if received on or after the date of bankruptcy.

Counterintuitively however, while specialist advice should always be obtained, it is often preferable to ensure no payments are received from superannuation until after a bankruptcy arrangement is entered into. This is because if payments are received by a member before bankruptcy the source of the funds may become merged or intermingled with other assets and no longer protected.

Anecdotally, there are situations where a trustee in bankruptcy has deliberately delayed a bankruptcy petition until after a member satisfies a condition of compulsory cashing in order to increase the prospects of a bankrupt's superannuation savings being available.

Similarly, the balance of a member's entitlements where they are in pension phase is generally protected. The income received by a member from pension payments are however assessed as income in the hands of the bankrupt.

This is important because under the Bankruptcy Act there are restrictions on how much income a bankrupt can earn before a proportion of the income is forfeited.

The formula used to determine the quantum of income that is paid to a trustee in bankruptcy is:

$$\frac{\text{Assessed income, less the income threshold}}{2}$$

'Assessed income' is essentially a bankrupt's gross income, less all tax (including Medicare).

The income threshold for a bankrupt is determined with reference to their dependants and is indexed regularly.

A detailed analysis of bankruptcy is outside the scope of this book, however the author has published a book titled 'The Nine Foundations of Asset Protection' which addresses all relevant issues in detail.

Notional estate provisions

A wider asset protection issue in relation to SMSFs and estate planning relates to the notional estate provisions that currently only apply in New South Wales.

Laws in each state of Australia allow a family member or certain other dependants to challenge a deceased's will. Such a claim is generally known as either a family provision application or a TFM claim.

Whether a TFM claim is successful, depends upon a range of matters—regardless of the outcome, however, TFMs can be costly and emotionally debilitating for all parties involved.

Historically in all Australian states, a TFM claim could only relate to property that was owned by the deceased on the date of their death, putting certain property such as SMSF assets, trust assets or those owned by a will maker's spouse outside the reach of a TFM claim.

In New South Wales however, special rules allow the courts to make orders in relation to assets that do not in fact form part of a deceased's personal estate.

In many respects, the rules are analogous to those under the Bankruptcy Act in that will makers who take steps to remove assets from their personal name leave those assets exposed to be 'clawed back' into the estate for the purposes of family provision applications made within 3 years of the date of their death.

While the rules apply to anyone living in New South Wales at the date of death, they also potentially apply where the will maker has any assets connected with New South Wales. This means that, in relation to SMSFs, the following situations may be exposed:

a If there is one asset in the SMSF that has the necessary connection with New South Wales (e.g. a house), that may be sufficient to drag all assets of the SMSF into the New South Wales notional estate provisions.

b A company that is listed on the stock exchange, but happens to have its registered office in New South Wales, can be an asset that can be subject to the notional estate provisions automatically. Thus, even if an SMSF has no assets in New South Wales at all, but happens to own shares in a listed company that is registered in New South Wales, those shares are subject to the notional estate rules and again, all the other assets in the super fund are similarly exposed.

c Finally, if the trustee company of an SMSF is registered in New South Wales, even though the fund itself has no assets in New South Wales, this is sufficient to allow the New South Wales notional estate provisions to apply.

While there have to date been very few cases that have applied the notional estate provisions, each of the above possibilities should be taken into account by any member of an SMSF who is concerned that there estate planning arrangements may be challenged.

Chapter 4

DEATH BENEFITS

Overview

A superannuation death benefit is a payment received from an SMSF because of the death of a person who was a member of that fund.

Death benefits do not automatically form part of a person's estate.

Rather, an analysis of the legislation, the SMSFs trust deed, relevant case law and in some instances, the manner in which the fund is controlled, need to be considered to determine how the superannuation death benefits should be paid.

Eligible recipients

Under section 62 of the SIS Act, a death benefit can only be paid to:

a a 'dependant' of the person; or
b the member's LPR, being the executors or administrators of their estate.

Dependants

The definition of 'dependant' is contained in section 10 of the SIS Act and includes:

a the spouse of the person;
b any child of the person; and
c any person with whom the person has an 'interdependency' relationship.

Under section 10A of the SIS Act, two persons have an interdependency relationship if:

a they have a close personal relationship;
b they live together;
c one or each of them provides the other with financial support; and
d one or each of them provides the other with domestic support and personal care.

Two people may also have an interdependency relationship if they have a close personal relationship and the only reason they fail to satisfy all the conditions in section 10A of the SIS Act is that either or both of them suffer from a physical, intellectual or psychiatric disability.

There are a range of factors that may or may not be taken into account when determining whether an interdependency relationship exists, some of which are:

a the duration of the relationship;
b whether or not a sexual relationship exists;
c the ownership, use and acquisition of property;
d degree of mutual commitment to a shared life;
e care and support for children;
f the reputation and public aspects of the relationship;
g the degree of emotional support;

h the extent to which the relationship is one of mere convenience; and
i any evidence suggesting that the parties intend the relationship to be permanent.

The definition of 'dependant' also takes on its ordinary meaning and whilst there have been efforts in other contexts to give a very wide meaning to the term (for instance, to include emotional dependency), case law to date indicates that dependency in the superannuation context requires a degree of financial dependency.

The definition of dependant does not include grandchildren, unless the grandchild is financially dependent on the grandparent at the time of their death, or the member and the grandchild were in an interdependency relationship.

Therefore, generally a person cannot leave death benefits from their superannuation fund directly to a grandchild, however (as discussed in more detail below), they may pass the benefits to grandchildren or other non-dependants by nominating their LPR as the death benefit beneficiary and including specific gifts of the entitlements in their will.

Generally, children will not be in an interdependency relationship with their parents, however it may exist where:

a they have a close personal relationship, they live together and one or each of them provides the other with financial support; and
b one or each of them provides the other with support and care of a type and quality normally provided in a close personal relationship, rather than by a friend or flatmate.

Definition of LPR

LPR is defined in the SIS Act to include:

a the executor of the will;
b an administrator of the estate of a deceased person;
c the trustee of the estate of a person under a legal disability; and
d a person who holds an enduring power of attorney granted by a person.

LPR's are bound to pay the benefit in accordance with the terms of the deceased member's will, or if the member dies intestate in respect of the superannuation entitlement, then in accordance with the relevant intestacy rules.

Consequently, a will-maker may include a specific gift of their superannuation entitlements to one or more non-dependants, however the gift will only be effective if their entitlements first pass to their LPR, either as a result of a BDBN or the discretion of the SMSF trustee.

Form of payment

A person's death benefit may be paid out to a beneficiary as:

a one or more lump sums;
b one or more pensions; or
c a combination of the above.

However, only certain types of beneficiaries can receive particular types of benefits.

Under SIS regulation 6.21 (2A), a pension may only be paid to a dependant of the member, however if the dependant is a child of the member, the child must also be:

a under the age of 18;
b disabled under the Disability Services Act; or
c under the age of 25 and financially dependent on the deceased.

All other death benefit payments must take the form of a lump sum payment.

If a death benefit is paid in the form of a pension to the child of a deceased member where the child is under 25 and financially dependent on the deceased at the date of death of the member, it must be cashed as a lump sum no later than the time at which the child turns 25 (unless the child has a permanent disability).

The form of benefit that will be provided to a dependant can also create significant tax implications based on the type and mix of benefits chosen.

For example, it may be prudent to provide dependent children with a pension as they are taxed at adult rates. However, in the same context, it may not be appropriate to set aside a significant part of the death benefit to pay a pension to the child if that child must be paid the balance as a lump sum upon attaining the age of 25.

How soon is 'as soon as practicable'?

Regulation 6.21 of the SIS Regulations requires death benefits to be cashed 'as soon as practicable' following the death of a member.

Unfortunately, 'as soon as practicable' is not defined in the Regulations and has not been otherwise defined.

Generally in our experience the Tax Office has historically expected death benefits to be paid within 6 months of a person's death, or earlier if possible.

While perhaps not directly relevant, part of the reason for this approach is likely to be because under section 17A(4) of the SIS Act, any replacement trustee (or replacement director of a corporate trustee) must resign within 6 months of the death benefits commencing to be paid. In other words, 6 months is legislated in a manner that is arguably analogous to the concept of 'as soon as practicable'.

This said, if there are objectively reasonable circumstances preventing payment for more than 6 months, this is unlikely to cause a breach of the rules, so long as the payment occurs as soon as practicable once the relevant circumstances have been resolved.

Some examples of where a payment after 6 months may still meet the 'as soon as practicable' test include:

1. It may be that probate of a member's estate is seen as required before paying a death benefit, and generally probate will take longer than 6 months;
2. If there is a risk that an estate may be challenged or the potential recipients of a death benefit challenging the trustee's decision, confirming that the risk has passed will generally take longer than 6 months;
3. similarly, if there is an actual challenge to a deceased estate this may warrant delaying paying of a death benefit;
4. if there is uncertainty about the validity of any purported binding death benefit nomination this may take longer than 6 months to resolve;
5. the nature of the assets in a fund may make distributions within 6 months impossible, for example illiquid assets such as real estate or investments in platforms that have large penalties for early withdrawal;
6. it may also be that the values of assets that are will form part of the cashing take an extended period to value;
7. surrounding circumstances, such as poor health of a surviving fund member may also justify a payment commencing later than 6 months.

Interestingly, the 2017 superannuation reform legislation permits a reversionary beneficiary 12 months to decide if they wish to cash their benefit before it is automatically credited to their transfer balance. This allowance may (again by analogy) support the argument that a death benefits payment within 12 months will meet the 'as soon as practicable' test, even without other explanatory reasons.

Taxation of death benefits

The manner in which a death benefit is taxed will differ depending on a number of factors, including whether:

a the payment is a lump sum or a pension payment;
b it is made to a death benefit dependant or a non-dependant; and
c it comprises a tax free component or taxable component (or a proportion of both).

The definition of a 'death benefit dependant' is contained in the Tax Act and is different to the definition contained in the SIS Act.

A death benefit dependant of a person who has died is:

a the deceased person's spouse or former spouse;
b the deceased person's child aged less than 18;

c any other person with whom the deceased person had an interdependency relationship just before he or she died; or

d any other person who was a dependant of the deceased person just before he or she died.

'Interdependency relationship' has the same definition as in section 10A of the SIS Act.

The main difference between the SIS Act and Tax Act definitions of dependant is that the Tax Act does not consider a child over 18 to be a dependant unless they are disabled or they were under 25 and financially dependent on the deceased at the date of death.

Death benefits paid to adult children who do not otherwise qualify as tax dependants will be taxed on the payment as a non-dependant.

Importantly, it is only the taxable component of a benefit that is potentially subject to tax. The tax-free component (as the name would suggest) is always tax free in the recipient's hands, irrespective of whether the recipient is a dependant or non-dependant.

Lump Sum Payments

A lump sum death benefit payment made to a death benefit dependant will be tax free.

Where a dependant was originally receiving a pension and cashes out the balance of their entitlement as a result of turning 25, the lump sum payment will be tax free even though they do not fulfil the definition of a death benefit dependant under the Tax Act.

In relation to lump sum payments made to non-dependants, the taxation treatment depends upon whether the payment comprises a tax free component, a taxable component or a combination of both.

As noted above, the tax free component passes without taxation.

The tax free component includes contributions that have not been taxed (e.g. non-concessional contributions) and crystallised 30 June 2007 amounts (pre-July 83 component, undeducted contributions, post-30 June 1994 invalidity component, concessional component and CGT exempt component).

The balance of any payment will then be the taxable component. The taxable component then has two elements:

a the element taxed; and

b the element untaxed.

Although generally the taxable component will be comprised entirely of a taxed element, an untaxed element will arise if insurance is used to fund part of the death benefit.

The element taxed of a lump sum death benefit paid to a non-dependant is included in assessable income of the non-dependant, with a tax offset to ensure that the rate of tax on the element taxed does not exceed 15%.

The element untaxed of a lump sum death benefit paid to a non-dependant is included in assessable income with a tax offset to ensure that the rate of tax on the element untaxed in the fund does not exceed 30%.

As the Medicare levy applies to both the element taxed and element untaxed, the effective tax rates become 16.5% and 31.5% respectively.

Pension Payment

Income streams can only be paid to dependants.

The tax position in relation to pensions, with reference to the $1.6M transfer balance cap, is outlined above.

As is the case with lump sum benefits, the tax free component of a death benefit pension is tax free.

The following table outlines the tax treatment for the two elements of the taxable component on the payment to a dependant of an income stream or pension.

Description	Tax treatment
The dependant is aged 60 or over	Element taxed is tax free. Element untaxed is included in the dependant's assessable income. Dependant receives a 10% tax offset.
The deceased member is aged 60 or over and the dependant is any age	Element taxed is tax free. Element untaxed is included in the dependant's assessable income. Dependant receives a 10% tax offset.
Both the deceased member and the dependant are under 60	Element taxed is included in the dependant's assessable income. Dependant receives a 15% tax offset. Element untaxed is included in the dependant's assessable income.

Other considerations

In addition to the tax related issues outlined above, a number of rules are potentially relevant in the context of death and superannuation.

The four main issues in this regard are:

a the proportioning rule;
b the inability to pay pensions to non-dependants;
c the taxation treatment of benefits paid to non-dependant children; and
d payments via the estate, and the use of testamentary trusts.

Proportioning rule

The proportioning rule requires that any superannuation benefit when paid is taken to comprise tax free and taxable components in the same proportions as they bear to the member's superannuation entitlements.

Without this rule, when paying a death benefit there would be an incentive to distribute:

a tax-free components to non-tax dependants; and
b taxable components to tax dependants.

The rule effectively results in the taxable portion of the death benefit that is paid to a non-tax dependant being subject to tax.

The only way in which this outcome can be avoided within a single fund is to ensure all payments are made to death benefit dependants.

An alternative approach is commonly referred to as the 're-contribution strategy' and involves:

a establishing a second fund for the member during their lifetime;
b ensuring that only contributions, transfers and roll-overs which would give rise to a tax-free component are made to the new fund, while all other contributions are made to the existing fund; and
c over time, withdrawing funds from the first fund (either as lump sums or as a pension) and making after-tax contributions to the second fund.

As the second fund is comprised of almost entirely tax-free components (the earnings in the fund will create a taxable component), this fund can then be used to pay death benefits to non-tax dependants.

Obviously this approach will not work in all cases, and requires the establishment of a second fund with the associated administrative costs. The strategy can however provide some scope to at least reduce the tax that non-dependants might otherwise incur if a single fund approach was adopted.

It should be noted that separate and distinct funds are required for this approach, as the ATO does not accept that separate accounts within the same superannuation fund have the benefit of separate treatment under the proportioning rule.

The application of the general anti-avoidance rules under part IVA of the Tax Act also need to be considered.

As also noted above, the effectiveness of this type of strategy that relies on recontributing to superannuation has been undermined by the limitation on contributions from 1 July 2017.

No pensions to non-dependants

The requirement to pay lump sums to non-tax dependants coupled with the proportioning rule ensures that tax will always be payable on the taxable component of a death benefit paid to a non-tax dependant.

In this context, a child who does not qualify for receipt of a pension as set out above cannot be paid a pension, even if the child otherwise qualifies as a tax dependant.

Therefore, even where a member is fully supporting an adult child, unless that child is considered disabled under the Disability Services Act (or is under 25 and financially dependent on the deceased member at the date of death), the child must take any benefit as a lump sum.

Although as a financial dependant a child will not be taxed on the lump sum benefit paid to them, the inability to take the benefit as a pension limits the availability of concessional tax treatment on the income stream. This is because any income stream derived by that child on investment of the lump sum benefit will be taxed in their hands at their marginal tax rate.

Non-dependent children

One of the well known anomalies with the payment of a death benefit is the difference in the tax treatment where a member aged 60 or over is able to 'predict' the timing of their death.

When a member is over 60 years of age, generally all super benefits will be tax-free on withdrawal prior to death.

In contrast, the same benefits distributed as a death payment can be liable for tax of up to 30% (plus Medicare and other surcharges).

Therefore, if the member of an SMSF knows exactly (or even approximately) when they will die, they would withdraw their entire benefit as a lump sum before death, pay no tax, and either pay the benefit to their child, or leave it to fall into their estate to be paid to the child under the will, or to their ultimate benefit via a testamentary trust.

On the other hand, where a member dies unexpectedly, the death benefit paid to that same child is subject to tax in the hands of the child as set out above.

This results in a de facto death duty being imposed on individuals who die unexpectedly, with adult children receiving their superannuation entitlements.

Obviously, there are a range of competing issues that need to be considered as part of any superannuation and estate planning exercise, however there seems to be an increasing trend for SMSF members to actively review the total amount they wish to retain in an SMSF in their later years.

For those wishing to limit the amount of tax payable on death, there is a bias to withdrawing amounts from superannuation fund prior to death.

This said, if a member withdraws too much, the contribution caps will limit how much (if any) they can re-contribute to superannuation and the income earned on investment outside super will not enjoy concessional tax treatment.

In particular, where a member withdraws their entire benefit as a lump sum, any earnings and subsequent capital gains on these investments will occur outside the super environment and will not be concessionally taxed—that is, they will be taxed at the marginal rates of tax. Where benefits are retained in the superannuation environment, with pensions continuing, any earnings, capital gains and pension payments will be tax-free.

While some advisers argue that it is possible to 'pre-sign' a super benefits withdrawal form to enable it to be dated by someone after the member's death (the date would be some time before death).

Practically however, and ignoring the question of fraud, the ATO requires physical withdrawal in order to avoid the imposition of tax and therefore 'pre-signing' withdrawal forms is an ineffective strategy.

Payments to the estate and testamentary trusts

Where a death benefit is paid to an estate (via the LPR), a 'look-through' approach is adopted and the tax treatment is largely the same as for direct payments.

In other words, the tax treatment depends upon who ultimately receives the benefit from the estate—to the extent that tax dependants receive the benefit, it will be tax free.

Where non-tax dependants receive the benefit, it will be taxed according to the various components as set out above and the trustee of the estate will be liable to account for tax on the benefit.

If the entitlements pass to a testamentary trust, there is a risk the proceeds will be treated as passing to a non-dependant unless appropriate safeguards are in place.

Specifically, assuming the testamentary trust has a broad range of eligible beneficiaries (which may include both death benefit dependants and non-dependants), then the will should ideally include discretion for the trustee to segregate or quarantine the superannuation entitlements for the benefit of the death benefit dependants only.

Alternatively, the will could create multiple testamentary trusts with one testamentary trust being established specifically to receive the superannuation entitlements, again with the range of beneficiaries being limited to death benefit dependants of the will-maker.

As a third alternative, in some circumstances it might also be appropriate to have the death benefit paid directly death benefit dependants rather than the estate.

CGT and death benefit in specie distributions

Special consideration must be given to the succession issues around an SMSF where non-liquid assets such as real estate are owned.

The ownership of property via an SMSF can have many advantages, including:

a the members effectively pay rent to themselves, which is deductible to the payer. The SMSF enjoys concessional tax treatment, so the net income is taxed at a maximum rate of 15%;
b a limited recourse borrowing arrangement (as explained earlier) can be used to effectively allow the SMSF to borrow to fund the acquisition;
c any gain ultimately on the sale of the property will be taxed at a maximum rate of 10% (assuming the property has been held for 12 months); and
d once the member enters pension phase and the property is used to support the pension payment, no tax is payable on the net income or capital gain.

However issues commonly arise where an SMSF owns the business real property from which the members (or an entity they control) operate their business.

In particular, problems can arise if the member wishes to retain the property with a view to passing it to the next generation, such as where the business itself is intended to pass to the next generation.

The SIS Act requires a death benefit to be paid to a beneficiary. If the benefit can be paid, say, as a pension to the surviving spouse, this may delay the need in the short term to deal with the underlying asset. However, at some future point (on the death of the spouse), there will be a need to deal with the asset.

If member dies in pension phase and their pension pass to a dependant beneficiary, then the dependant may either:

a continue receiving pension payments tax free; or
b exercise their entitlement to a lump sum payment equal to the value of the underlying pension asset.

The alternative approach of transferring the asset to a beneficiary can cause a number of revenue related issues, including:

a there are no proceeds from the disposal of the asset, so the SMSF must find other resources to meet the tax liability;
b stamp duty will generally be payable. In a sale, stamp duty is usual paid by the purchaser. With an in specie transfer, the parties will need to decide who pays the stamp duty liability. Again this will have to be funded separately as there are no proceeds from disposal;
c depending on the circumstances of the beneficiary, there may be tax to pay on receipt of the property as a superannuation death benefit. Again, because no cash proceeds are received, this tax needs to be funded independently.

Having the beneficiary as a member (or making them a member after the deceased member's death) does potentially solve the problems outlined above. This approach will however only assist if there are sufficient other assets to pay the death benefit. If this is the case then the property could support the continuing member's benefit, with other assets being paid out.

The key requirement is that the death benefit be paid—members cannot simply leave the benefit in the SMSF indefinitely.

Meaning of 'cashed'

Ensuring an SMSF continues to satisfy the rules in relation trusteeship following a member's death can be problematic, particularly when specific strategies have not been implemented as part of a comprehensive estate plan.

Where an individual member dies the Law allows 6 months for an SMSF to ensure compliance. Often, for funds that are established as 2 member funds, this is achieved via the appointment of a corporate trustee, with the remaining member as the sole director.

The Law also allows a grace period for non-compliance from the date of death until just before the death benefits commence to be paid, where the LPR can act as the replacement trustee.

Most modern SMSF trust deeds reflect the Law and have a discretionary provision that automatically appoints the LPR as the trustee on the death of the member. While there can be confusion about the way the rules work, the conservative position is that the 6 month grace period starts on the death of the member.

Therefore, regardless of when the death benefit commences to be paid, the trusteeship must be valid no later than 6 months following the date of a member's death.

In this context it is important to understand, as noted earlier, that a member's benefits must be 'cashed as soon as practicable' after the death of a member, which is set out under regulation 6.21(1) of the Law.

In particular, the question is whether a death benefit can be simply transferred to a surviving member's account by way of journal entry.

In this regard, in most other areas of the law, where two parties owe mutual liabilities or obligations, they can be set off the liabilities against each other through a book entry(being the so called 'rule in Spargo's case).

The ATO has confirmed that the principle in Spargo's case can also apply to SMSFs where there are mutual liabilities between the relevant fund and another party (see ATO ID 2015/2).

However the ATO has also confirmed in ATO ID 2015/3 however that a death benefit cannot be satisfied simply by way of journal entry, as death benefit dependants do not owe anything to the fund, that is there is no mutual liability to set off against the SMSF.

Therefore, death benefits must actually be paid to the death benefit dependant by the transfer of ownership of assets out of the SMSF.

The ATO also confirms that the Law does not allow for payments to be made to members by way of journal entry.

In particular, regulation 6.17(2) requires payments to be transferred out of the SMSF.

Unfortunately, this requirement for formal payment can in a practical sense trigger unnecessary transaction costs as well as complicating and delaying the death benefit payment process.

The quote from Spargo's case that is most often referred to is set out in full below -

> *'Nothing is clearer than that if parties account with each other, and sums are stated to be due on one side, and sums to an equal amount due on the other side on that account, and those accounts settled by both parties, it is exactly the same thing as if the sums due on both sides had been paid. Indeed, it is a general rule of law, that in every case where a transaction resolves itself with paying money by A to B, and then handing it back again by B to A, if the parties meet together and agree to set one demand against the other, they need not go through the form and ceremony of handing the money backwards and forwards.'*

SPTs

A SPT is a trust that is established solely to receive the superannuation benefits of a member following death. A SPT can be established by a will or by deed after the death of an individual.

Generally, the beneficiaries of a SPT must be confined to persons who are 'death benefit dependants' of the deceased, as explained above.

The benefits of having a SPT in a will are:

a it provides greater asset protection compared to the superannuation death benefits being paid directly to a death benefit dependant—for example, against relationship breakdowns, creditors or spendthrift beneficiaries;

b distributions from the SPT will generally be 'excepted trust income' –this means that recipients under the age of 18 will be treated as adults for tax purposes;

c the distribution of the superannuation death benefits to the SPT is taxed in the same way as if they had been paid directly to the death benefit dependant (provided the beneficiaries of the SPT are limited to tax dependants).

Generally, most advisers draft the terms of testamentary trusts such that the range of potential beneficiaries listed are significantly wider than dependants for tax purposes. Specialist advisers will however also generally craft the testamentary trust so that the trustee has complete discretion about which of the beneficiaries may receive any superannuation benefits available for distribution.

In particular, the terms of the will allow the trustee to essentially establish a 'sub trust' of the testamentary trust for receipt of the superannuation proceeds—with the only beneficiaries being those who satisfy the definition of a tax dependant.

In this way, the various benefits of having a SPT, as outlined above, can be achieved.

To ensure that any receipt of superannuation proceeds is tax-free, the LPR should ensure that, at least at the time of receipt of the superannuation proceeds by the SPT, the only capital beneficiaries of the SPT are individuals who meet the definition of 'death benefit dependant' under s 302-195 of the Tax Act.

In practical terms, this means that where there is more than one death benefit dependant, the terms of the SPT should provide that they receive the trust capital in specified shares on vesting.

ATO Interpretative Decision 2001/751 (which has been withdrawn on the basis that its view has been subsumed into s 302-10 of the ITAA 1997) confirms that it appears to be the clear intention of the legislation that the fact that a payment is made to a trustee, rather than directly to the dependant, should not obscure the fact that the payment is ultimately for the benefit of the dependant.

In the facts considered in ATO ID 2001/751, the death benefit dependant was the sole beneficiary of the trust and, therefore, absolutely entitled to the income and capital of the trust.

For completeness, as superannuation proceeds do not automatically form part of the estate of the deceased member, it may be necessary to ensure that appropriate nominations are made by the member to direct that the superannuation death benefits are paid to the LPR for distribution under the will, and if appropriate, to any SPT established.

If the trustee chooses to utilise a SPT, an example of how the estate assets could flow is as follows:

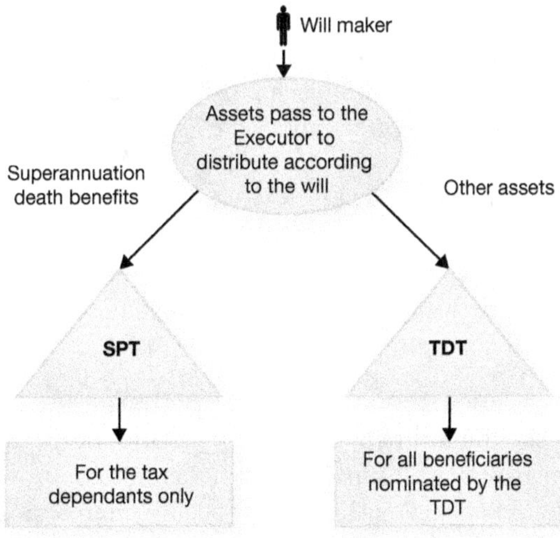

SPTs established outside a will

SPTs may also be established outside a will, after the death of a will maker, where the deceased's will does not contain a testamentary trust with the features mentioned above. This style of SPT is of particular benefit to a surviving spouse with infant children, where tax effective income splitting is important.

For example:

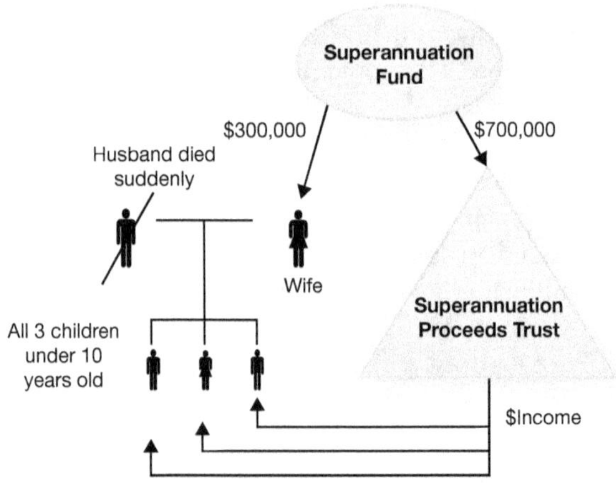

Following the death of the husband, the wife in default of any other decision by the trustee of the SMSF would be entitled to receive his $1 million superannuation death benefit.

The wife, in her capacity as trustee of the SMSF distributes $700,000 to a SPT she establishes and controls.

Income and capital distributions to the infant children can then be used to pay for food, accommodation, school fees, clothing, holidays etc.

Each year the wife is able to distribute approximately $22,000 to each of the three children (i.e. over $65,000) tax free, under the excepted trust income rules of the Tax Act.

There are a number of technical provisions that need to be satisfied to ensure access to this outcome.

Generally, an SPT established following the death of a member of an SMSF is significantly more restrictive than an SPT established pursuant to the terms of the former member's will, for example:

a minor beneficiaries (persons under 18 years of age on establishment of the SPT) must be the ultimate capital beneficiaries of the SPT, meaning the assets of the trust must ultimately vest in them;

b the transfer of benefits must generally occur within 3 calendar years of the date of death of the deceased;

c the concessional rates of tax will generally not be available to the grandchildren of a member; and

d depending on the situation, the assets transferred must not exceed the entitlements that the minor beneficiaries would have received if the deceased SMSF member had not left a valid will (i.e. if the deceased had died intestate).

SPTs are generally a structure of last resort. This is for a combination of reasons, not least of which because under superannuation law there is no clear pathway to allow a superannuation trustee to distribute to a SPT. Furthermore, unless the money passes directly from the superannuation fund into the SPT, there is a real risk that the ATO will not allow access to the excepted trust income provisions.

For these reasons it is usually preferable that the funds are paid to the LPR and then distributed under the will into a testamentary trust which is crafted in a way to create a 'sub-trust' in relation to the superannuation proceeds.

This approach ensures that the surviving spouse will have the flexibility to have all funds in a trust environment while also ensuring the proceeds are received tax free into the estate.

Use of nominations

As outlined above, death benefits do not automatically form part of a person's estate.

Rather, the trustee of the member's superannuation fund is responsible for the distribution of death benefits.

A member can regulate the manner in which their entitlements are paid in two ways:

a through the use of death benefit nominations; or

b by regulating control of the SMSF, thereby determining who will have the discretion to pay the death benefits following the member's death.

c In virtually every estate planning exercise, the issue of how members of an SMSF can direct payment of benefits, on death, invariably arises.

d Essentially a member of an SMSF has three main choices for specifying what should happen in relation to their superannuation entitlements on death (assuming the proposed recipient is entitled at law), namely:

    (i) nomination—the trustee is bound to deal with a member's benefit in their best interests. Before making a decision, the trustee will normally make enquiries as to the member's family situation, who their dependants are, the provisions of their will and other relevant circumstances;

    (ii) a non-BDBN—the trustee is not bound by a non-binding notice and has an absolute discretion as to where the death benefit will be paid.

Where a non-binding notice is made, it should be taken into account as part of any decision by the trustee as to how to distribute the benefit; and

(iii) a BDBN—the trustee is obliged to distribute a member's death benefits in accordance with a valid BDBN.

BDBNs have the potential to allow members to protect their death benefits from disputes; where there is no nomination or a non-binding one, a trustee's decision can be challenged.

BDBNs can also be used as part of a member's overall estate plan—for example, as part of a tax planning strategy for infant children or as an asset protection strategy for adult children.

A BDBN is essentially an election made by a member that is binding on the trustee, whereby the trustee agrees to direct any benefits remaining in a member's superannuation account in the way that the member has instructed.

If the trust fund of the SMSF allows it, a member may make a BDBN. The trustee is legally bound to comply with a valid BDBN. That is the trustee has no discretion to pay death benefits other than in accordance with the notice.

A BDBN must be made strictly in compliance with the requirements of the relevant trust deed to be effective and if the trust deed does not permit BDBNs, any purported BDBN by the member is unlikely to be upheld by a Court if challenged.

Below is an example of some of the requirements that are generally set out in a trust deed as needing to be satisfied before a nomination will be held to be binding (the first three of which are expressly required by legislation):

'*Any binding death benefit nomination:*

a *must be in writing;*
b *must be signed and dated by the member in the presence of two adult witnesses;*
c *must contain a declaration signed and dated by the witnesses that the member signed the notice in their presence;*
d *will not lapse with the passing of time;*
e *may be revoked by the member by written notice to the trustee at any time;*
f *must contain sufficient details to identify the member; and*
g *must contain sufficient details to identify the beneficiaries.*'

While almost all trust deeds that allow BDBNs will have provisions along the lines outlined above, at times there will be additional provisions that are not necessarily expected. Some examples in this regard can include:

a a prohibition on amending the trust deed for the SMSF in a way that impacts on the BDBN;
b a provision that empowers the trustee to accept amended BDBNs from the financial attorney of a member;

c the trustee may be required to consider and accept a BDBN before it is valid; and
d there may be a particular table or form that is required to be embedded into the BDBN, which sets out the percentage entitlement of each beneficiary.

Although BDBNs can provide greater certainty to members of where their superannuation is to be distributed once they die, they also create a lack of flexibility, particularly for any change in circumstances.

For instance, a BDBN may result in unfavourable tax outcomes for the beneficiaries if it is not reviewed and updated following changes to the tax laws affecting death benefits.

In addition, a BDBN is only binding on the trustee if the death benefits are directed to the member's LPR or dependants.

Historically, BDBNs expired after 3 years if they were not confirmed and in many funds, this is still the case. More recent deeds however allow non-lapsing BDBNs to be made, which will continue indefinitely unless expressly revoked by the member.

If a BDBN expires without being renewed, the trustee is free to distribute the relevant money any way they like (so long as it is permitted under the fund's deed and superannuation law).

As is the case with wills, BDBNs should also be updated or confirmed when there is a significant change in a person's circumstances, such as divorce, death and additional children.

A non-binding death benefit nomination, as its name suggests, does not obligate a trustee to make a payment and are merely a guide. The trustee retains a discretion (subject to the terms of the deed) as to how the death benefit is paid.

The main disadvantage of a BDBN is the inability of a trustee to rectify the situation where the member has not kept the nomination up to date, particularly where there has been a significant change in the circumstances of the member.

If a member is unlikely to keep their nomination up to date, a non-BDBN allows the trustee to consider these factors in deciding how the death benefit should be paid and is often more appropriate.

When should a BDBN be used?

One issue that arises regularly is when should a BDBN be used.

Broadly, a BDBN will be useful in the following circumstances:

a people in second or third marriages;
b where there are children from different relationships;
c where there are concerns about beneficiaries challenging the estate;
d if the relevant entitlements are held in an industry fund (as opposed to an SMSF) and there is a risk that a trustee may make a decision that does not reflect the member's wishes.

The main advantage of making a BDBN is the certainty it provides.

By completing a BDBN the risk of challenges to the fund that might arise on the member's death are minimised.

The main disadvantage of making a BDBN, particularly for SMSFs, is that the nomination locks the trustee into directing any death benefits to the dependants or to the LPR nominated.

If a person's circumstances change, for instance, due to divorce, separation or bankruptcy, the certainty that was hoped for might be negated. Similarly, if the laws change a BDBN can be extremely ineffective.

Therefore, unless there is a compelling reason for a BDBN to be implemented, it is generally preferred at least for SMSFs that a non-binding nomination be implemented, or no nomination at all. This then allows the trustee to make a decision that is optimal in all the circumstances at the date of the member's death. Often this is for the benefit to be paid to the member's estate to be distributed to a testamentary trust set up under their will.

A few critical points to remember in this area include the following –

a If a member's circumstances change and they have failed to update their BDBN, it will, subject in some situations to automatic lapsing (for example, every three years), continue to be binding on the trustee.

b The trust deed for an SMSF must allow for a BDBN to be given to the trustee of the fund—even some recently set up deeds do not always have such a provision.

c Unless specifically provided for in the SMSF trust deed, a BDBN will often need to be 'refreshed' every three years. An alternate approach is to update the trust deed for the SMSF to 'hardwire' the nomination into the deed, avoiding the requirement to regularly refresh the nomination (often referred to as a 'superannuation will').

d Where this is done, the fact that there might be other nominations, or even provisions in a person's will, are of no effect—rather the terms of the SMSF trust deed must be followed.

Superannuation wills

Another approach, similar to BDBNs is the use of 'superannuation wills'.

This terminology can be somewhat misleading as the document is not a 'will' in the ordinary meaning, and different organisations can be referring to different approaches when they refer to 'superannuation wills'.

In general however, a 'superannuation will' involves amending the trust deed for the SMSF to embed the nomination of beneficiaries within that document, rather than relying on a stand-alone nomination.

For instance, the trust deed may be amended to specify that a particular member's death benefits must be paid to their LPR upon the death.

The deed will then commonly also contain provisions preventing any amendments from being made to the death benefit provisions of the deed, after a member's death.

This approach is only available for SMSFs and can be very inflexible (if a member later wishes to vary their nomination, the entire deed must be amended), however in the appropriate circumstances it can be a powerful tool for ensuring the member's wishes are followed.

The 'read the deed' mantra, which is so often used in the context of family trusts, is of similar importance in relation to superannuation wills. One particular provision to be aware of in this regard is that, even if a nomination (which appears to be binding) is embedded under the SMSF trust deed, unless the provision of that deed has a prohibition against amendment, the intentions of the parties may not in fact be achieved.

For example, the remaining trustees after death could elect to vary the SMSF trust deed (and effectively remove the BDBN) before ultimately making a death benefit payment as they determine.

There are a number of limitations surrounding what actions an attorney can take on behalf of a donor under an enduring power of attorney.

One transaction that is not dealt with expressly in the superannuation or attorney legislation is whether a BDBN can be made, changed, revoked or refreshed.

The conservative position is that any step in relation to a BDBN is a personal power, and therefore cannot be delegated to an attorney.

This said, the preferred view seems to be that so long as the attorney is given power under the enduring power of attorney, and the trust deed for the superannuation fund does not otherwise contain any prohibitions, then an attorney may take steps in relation to a BDBN, so long as they believe that it is in the best interests of the donor.

This line of reasoning is supported by SCT determination No. D-7-084/030.

> *It also appears to be relatively widely accepted that an attorney may be able to 'affirm' an existing BDBN that has lapsed, again so long as there is an express power in the attorney appointment document.*

Specific asset BDBNs

One issue that can arise in relation to BDBNs is whether a BDBN can apply to specific assets, as opposed to simply nominating a percentage of total assets, which is the standard approach for most nominations.

The generally accepted position seems to be that given there is nothing in the superannuation legislation that prevents distributing specific assets under a BDBN, so long as the trust deed for the fund does not prohibit it, the approach is permissible.

If a specific asset BDBN is desired, it will also be necessary to ensure practical issues such as the following are addressed:

a the relevant asset must be segregated to the account of the member making the BDBN;
b compliance with all aspects of the BDBN rules under the trust deed;
c the various issues that should be factored into any BDBN, including changes in the values of assets, the wider estate plan, what is to occur if the intended recipient predeceases the person making the BDBN and the revenue consequences;
d finally, the scenario where the asset the subject of the specific asset BDBN is sold prior to the member's death should also be contemplated.

Reversionary pensions

Where a member has reached preservation age, and is already receiving their superannuation benefit as an income stream, it is possible to nominate a reversionary beneficiary that requires upon the member's death, that the income stream continues to be paid as they have directed.

Historically, the ATO sought to argue that a pension (and the tax exemption thereon) ceased as soon as the member in receipt of the pension died.

The exception to this position was where a dependent beneficiary of the deceased was automatically entitled under the super fund's deed, or rules of the pension, to receive the pension on the death of the member. This type of pension is often referred to as an ARP.

The Federal Government, however, announced that, with effect from 1 July 2012, a tax exemption applies following the death of an SMSF member in receipt of a pension until that pension has been paid out of the fund. The main requirement for the exemption to apply is that the pension is paid out of the fund as soon as practicable.

As a result, an ARP is not required to ensure access to the tax exemption.

Some confusion can also arise where a member has put in place both an ARP and a BDBN, with conflicting outcomes.

In these circumstances, the provisions of the trust deed are critical for determining whether the ARP or the BDBN should prevail, and it will often be the case that the ARP will take precedence over an inconsistent BDBN.

Where there is a BDBN in place for superannuation savings that are also the subject of a reversionary pension, it will be necessary to determine which takes priority.

Best practice dictates that both documents articulate which has priority, or at least that whichever document is signed most recently applies.

Where however there is limited guidance addressing the issue, it is generally accepted that the reversionary pension will take precedence over the BDBN. A key reason for this is because a valid reversionary pension would automatically remove the deceased member's death benefits from a fund, and therefore, any BDBN will have no assets to attach to.

In the absence of a clear answer in the legal documents, the ATO's position appears to have been confirmed via a National Tax Liaison Group (Superannuation Technical Sub-group) in March 2010.

The minutes confirm as follows:

> *'There are no SIS Act or SISR provisions that are relevant to determining which nomination an SMSF trustee is to give precedence where a deceased pension member had both a valid reversionary nomination and a valid BDBN in existence at the same time of the member's death.*
>
> *While section 59 of the SIS Act and Regulation 6.17A of the SISR place restrictions on superannuation entity trustees accepting BDBNs from a member, as explained in SMSF Determination SMSFD 2008/3, the Commissioner is of the view that those provisions do not have any application to SMSFs.*
>
> *It must also be remembered that section 59 of the SIS Act and regulation 6.17A of the SISR are necessary because of the general trust law principle that beneficiaries cannot direct trustees in the performance of their trust.*
>
> *The ATO's view is that a pension that is a genuine reversionary pension, that is, one which under the terms and conditions established at the commencement of the pension reverts to a nominated (or determinable) beneficiary must be paid to the reversioner.*
>
> *It is only where a trustee may exercise its discretion as to which beneficiary is paid the deceased member's benefits and/or the form in which the benefits are payable that a death benefit nomination is relevant.'*

Are 'life interest' pensions possible?

There has been ongoing debate in recent years about the ability for a 'life interest' pension to be created—that is for a pension to be paid by a super fund to a person for their life, before then reverting automatically to beneficiaries of the original pension owner.

The conservative view tends to be that the balance of any reversionary pension passes as directed by the reversionary pensioner on their death, not the original pensioner.

The reasons for this conclusion include that there are no legislative provisions that directly and categorically support the ability to create life interest pensions.

Furthermore, the initial pensioner's deceased estate (being the intended recipient on the death of the life tenant pensioner) would not technically be an income stream dependant under the Law and is therefore ineligible to receive any pension.

The initial pensioner's children would also not be potential income stream dependants (unless they under 18 years old, financially dependent or under a disability), and therefore would also not be eligible to receive pensions.

The risks of a fund not technically being in pension phase include that it would not be tax exempt on the income stream paid, the pension terms and related documents may be invalid and penalties may be imposed. Practically, it may also mean that the life interest pensioner can simply ignore the purported terms of the pension.

Another aspect supporting the conservative view that life interest pensions are at best a risky approach relates to the requirement under the Law (namely regulation 6.21) that death benefit payments are made 'as soon as practicable' following a member's death.

In order for a life interest pension to achieve its objective, on the death of the second pensioner the capital must form part of the initial pensioner's death benefits not the life interest pensioner on their death. The death benefits would then be paid to the initial pensioner's dependants or legal personal representative.

Arguably, a payment that does not take place until the life interest pensioner has died will not meet the 'as soon as practicable' requirement.

If this argument is correct then not only would the purported payment be invalid, the life interest pensioner could simply ignore the pension terms and the remaining capital would form part of their estate.

The potential work arounds to deliver a similar outcome as a life interest pension include:

- a A standard life-interest in a will;
- b Implementing mutual wills;
- c Establishing two separate superannuation funds.

Each of the above alternatives however have a number of issues, many of which are often seen as more problematic than those that relate to life interest pensions.

Practically therefore some advisers will look to establish a life interest pension, and ensure that issues such as the following are addressed:

- a Placing a limit on the income able to be withdrawn by the life interest pensioner;
- b Restricting the life interest pensioner's rights as a trustee (or director of a corporate trustee), particularly in relation to any commutation of the reversionary pension;
- c 'Hardwiring' into the terms of the trust deed the exact way in which the remaining capital of the pension is to be paid on the death of the life interest pension and ensuring that these terms are 'double entrenched' to prevent them ever being amended;
- d Creating a 'third party approval' position, such as a 'guardian' or 'protector' who must provide prior written consent before certain steps (such as changing the trust deed in any way) are taken.

Chapter 5

KEY CASES

The issues which commonly arise when structuring an estate plan for superannuation benefits are highlighted in the following court decisions, summarised below.

Webb v Teeling [2009] FCA 1094

This case highlights an often over looked aspect of estate planning related to the payment of death benefits from a superannuation fund.

In general, when the beneficiary of a gift under a will dies after the willmaker but before the distribution has been made, that beneficiary (via their estate) will still be entitled to the gift.

Conversely however Webb v Teeling illustrates that this is not the case for superannuation benefits.

In summary the factual scenario was as follows:

- a a member of a super fund had passed away, validly nominating a dependant to receive the death benefit;
- b the dependant was alive at the time of the member's death;
- c the dependant subsequently died before the death benefit was paid and their LPR sought payment to the originally nominated beneficiary's estate.

It was held that the death benefit could not be paid to the LPR of the deceased dependant because they were neither:

- a a dependant of the deceased member; or
- b the deceased member's LPR.

With the aid of hindsight, the workaround in similar situations is to ensure that if the nominated beneficiary dies before the death benefit is paid, the funds should pass (ideally under a binding nomination) to the LPR of the member.

The member's will should then direct the amount specifically to the intended recipients and can do so without restriction as the superannuation rules will have been complied with by the initial payment to the member's LPR.

Malek (as Trustee for the Estate of Antoine Malek) v Federal Commissioner of Taxation (1999) 42 ATR

A potential recipient of a tax free superannuation death benefit includes someone who was financially dependent on the deceased just before they died.

While each situation will turn on the factual matrix, one of the leading cases in this area is Malek.

In this case, the relevant fund member was, at the time of his death, living with his widowed mother in a unit owned by her. The son contributed to paying most expenses, paid for repairs and alterations to the unit and a holiday for his mother.

Following the member's death, the Tax Office treated the mother's receipt of the death benefit payment (that flowed to her via the son's will) as taxable as she was not a dependant.

In reversing the Tax Office's decision it was confirmed –

> '... *the relevant financial support (to create financial dependency) is that required to maintain the person's normal standard of living and the question of fact to be answered is whether the alleged dependant was reliant on the regular continuous contribution of the other person to maintain that standard.*'

Here, it was clear that the requisite level of dependency existed and therefore the mother was entitled to receive the death benefit payment tax free.

Katz v Grossman [2005] NSWSC 934

Although from 2005, one of the most famous cases in this area remains Katz v Grossman.

The case highlights how important it is to ensure an appropriate trustee is appointed for an SMSF and how control of the SMSF should be one of the specific issues identified for consideration when reviewing an estate plan.

The case involved Katz bringing an action against his sister Grossman (and her husband), claiming an interest in their father's SMSF.

The facts were as follows:

- a the mother and father were the original individual trustees and members of the SMSF;
- b the mother died some years before the father, and subsequently Grossman (the daughter) was appointed as a co-trustee with her father to ensure that the SMSF continued to comply with the relevant superannuation legislation;
- c when the father subsequently died, Grossman appointed her husband as a co-trustee with her;
- d prior to his death, the father had made a non-BDBN indicating that he wanted his superannuation entitlements divided equally between Katz (his son) and Grossman;
- e the father's will also divided all his assets equally between Katz and Grossman; and
- f Grossman (and her husband) ignored the nomination and will and paid the entire superannuation entitlements, totalling approximately $1 million, to herself.

The Court held that:

- a all the trustees of the SMSF had been validly appointed at the relevant times;
- b as the nomination signed by the father was a non-BDBN, the trustee was entitled to elect not to follow it; and

c the trustee therefore had full discretion to determine how the entitlements should be paid, including the discretion to pay the full amount to Grossman to the exclusion of Katz.

As a result, the challenge by Katz was unsuccessful and Grossman was entitled to keep the superannuation entitlements, notwithstanding the father's apparent intention that Katz and Grossman share equally in all his assets, including the superannuation benefits.

Moss Super Pty Ltd v Hayne [2008] VSC 158

This case involved a dispute around an attempted change of trustee of an SMSF following the death of a member.

In particular, the surviving member purported to change the trusteeship of the SMSF, so that a company of which she was the sole shareholder and director would be appointed.

The trust deed set out the process by which a change of trusteeship could take place and specifically required the 'founder' to appoint any new trustee.

While the sole director of the new trustee company was also the founder, she did not in fact sign the change of trustee documentation in her capacity as founder.

In other words, while she signed in her capacity as the sole director of the new trustee, there was no provision where she also signed in her founder role.

Critically, the Court found that where structures are created in which individuals have multiple roles to play, the requirements around those roles must be respected and complied with. This meant the attempted change of trusteeship was invalid.

Notaras v Notaras [2012] NSWSC 947

In this case, two brothers were the trustees and members of an SMSF.

Over time, one of the brothers (Brinos) made withdrawals from the SMSF, of which around $60,000 were alleged to be in excess of his entitlement.

Brinos' brother (Basil) had no knowledge of the withdrawals and thus had not provided consent.

Basil approached the Court to seek an order that Brinos be removed as the trustee of the SMSF due to his failure to act jointly, and that he be replaced with a corporate trustee (Bazport Pty Ltd), of which Basil was the sole director and secretary.

The Court accepted Basil's argument appointed Bazport Pty Ltd as the co-trustee in place of Brinos, leaving the SMSF with both an individual and corporate trustee.

The Court confirmed Basil would (as a result of the decision) need approval from the Tax Office for its failure to comply with the superannuation law requirement for all members of an SMSF to also be trustees.

Ioppolo & Hesford v Conti & Anor [2013] WASC 389

Ioppolo v Conti provides another example of how unintended consequences can arise where the control of an SMSF is not properly considered as part of a member's estate plan.

The situation was as follows:

- a the husband and wife originally established an SMSF and were the individual trustees;
- b the wife died and left a will directing her LPR to pay her superannuation benefits to her children. The will specifically excluded her husband from receiving those benefits;
- c the wife had not signed any form of binding or non-binding death benefit nomination prior to her death;
- d following the wife's death, the husband retired as trustee and appointed a corporate trustee in his place. He was the sole director and shareholder of the corporate trustee; and
- e the corporate trustee then resolved to pay the entirety of the wife's superannuation entitlements (of approximately $650,000) to the husband, as opposed to her LPR pursuant to her will.

The executors of the will challenged the distribution and argued that the husband failed to act in a 'bona fide manner' in light of the provision in the will. They claimed that the husband should have appointed the executors as replacement trustees for the SMSF, rather than the corporate trustee with himself as the sole director.

The Court dismissed the executor's claim and allowed the husband to retain all of the wife's superannuation entitlements.

The Court confirmed that there is no obligation under the superannuation legislation for a surviving trustee to automatically appoint the executors of a former co-trustee as replacement trustees of an SMSF.

In addition, of particular relevance to advisers, the Court specifically noted that:

- a the husband had sought specialist advice in relation to his rights and obligations as the trustee;
- b the husband had deliberately waived his right to confidentiality (or privilege) in relation to this advice;
- c the Court on reviewing the advice agreed with the conclusion given, being that the husband was able to make the payment to himself;
- d where a trustee is acting on the advice of a specialist, it will generally be very difficult to successfully argue that the trustee lacked good faith in making the decision; and
- e ultimately, a Court will only review the way in which the discretion of a trustee is exercised in very limited circumstances.

Wooster v Morris [2013] VSC 594

Wooster v Morris explores some of the key issues around the enforceability of a **BDBN**.

The facts of the case were as follows:

a a husband and wife were the trustees and members of an SMSF;
b the husband had two adult daughters from a previous relationship;
c the husband had made a BDBN in favour of his adult daughters, who were also the executors of his will;
d the husband's wife, following his death, sought to challenge the BDBN on the basis that the trust deed required it to be delivered to her and she claimed that it had not been;
e as the wife was the sole surviving trustee and was able to regulate the appointment of the new trustee (ignoring the claims of the daughters as executors of the will), she paid the entire death benefit (being approximately $925,000) to herself.

The husband's daughters challenged the distribution and the Court ultimately ordered the wife to return all funds.

The Court also ordered the wife to contribute personally to the costs of the litigation (which were in the vicinity of $350,000), as these costs would otherwise have significantly depleted the balance of the superannuation entitlements being received by the adult daughters.

McIntosh v McIntosh [2014] QSC 99

The facts of this case were:

a a father and mother had a son, James, prior to their separation. By all reports, the relationship between the father and mother was acrimonious following the separation;
b James died without a will, meaning his parents were entitled to his estate in equal shares under the intestacy rules;
c his mother applied for and was granted letters of administration;
d James had around $450,000 in a superannuation fund and did not have a valid binding death benefit nomination at the date of his death, although he had a non-BDBN in favour of his mother;
e his mother applied to the trustee of the superannuation fund to have the entitlements paid to herself absolutely, rather than to herself in her capacity as administrator of the estate. This meant his mother would receive 100% of the entitlements, rather than the 50% she would have received from the estate; and
f his father challenged the mother's actions and argued that she was breaching her obligations as administrator to maximise the value of the estate.

The Court found in the father's favour and held that the mother had clear fiduciary duties as administrator to act in the best interests of the estate, and she had failed these duties by preferring her own interests over those of the estate.

The Court ordered the mother to pay the superannuation entitlements to the estate.

While there are obviously a number of issues in relation to this case, three critical steps that could have been taken are as follows:

- a To the extent that they were available, BDBNS could have been made to the mother personally (in this regard, non-BDBNs had in fact been made nominating the mother solely).
- b With the aid of hindsight, the mother should not have applied to administer the deceased estate. This would have relieved her of any duty to act in the best interests of the estate and therefore she could have proceeded to make the application for superannuation benefits to be paid to her personally without her actions being challenged.
- c The son should have made a will at least appointing his mother as executor (this would have potentially meant that she did not have any conflict of interest as the son would have been deemed to have been aware of the potential when making the nomination). Ideally, the will would have also nominated the mother as the sole beneficiary of the estate—thereby meaning that even if the funds were not paid to her directly, she should have ultimately received them in any event.

Whether the superannuation death benefits can be regulated via a will was considered by the SCT in D11-12/066 where the deceased failed to execute a BDBN or a non-BDBN.

Instead she executed a will which appointed her spouse, son and daughter as LPR and left a specific bequest to her spouse.

The trustee of the fund was of the opinion that in the absence of a BDBN, the entire superannuation benefit had to be paid to the LPR of the deceased, to be distributed in accordance with the terms of the will.

The deceased's spouse challenged this decision arguing that it was unfair and unreasonable given the deceased had left a specific bequest in her will to her. The spouse argued that this bequest constituted a death benefit direction.

The SCT found that the decision of the trustee to distribute the superannuation benefit to the deceased's LPR was not unfair, unreasonable or contrary to law. The trustee's decision was in accordance with the terms of the deed and the superannuation law and this, according to the SCT, was the correct decision.

The decision highlights the importance of standalone nominations and that it is unlikely a provision in a will can ever constitute a valid nomination.

Brine v Carter [2015] SASC 205

The decision in *Brine* provides another example of the key issues that need to be considered by LPRs, who are also potential beneficiaries of a superannuation death benefit.

In summary, the factual scenario was as set our below.

The deceased appointed his de facto partner and three children from an earlier relationship as his LPR.

The de facto made an application for the superannuation death benefits to be paid to her directly, as opposed to the estate.

If the superannuation proceeds had been paid to the estate, the three children would have been entitled.

For a period of time prior to the death benefit being paid, the de facto partner withheld details of the superannuation death benefit from the three children.

Importantly however, by the time the super fund trustee exercised its discretion, the three children were aware of all relevant information concerning the death benefits and had themselves made an application for the death benefits to be paid to the estate.

It was held that this was a critical point, that is, the other LPRs had effectively consented to the de facto making her individual claim by themselves making a claim on behalf of the estate in full knowledge of all relevant circumstances.

While the decision of the superannuation fund to pay the entitlements to the de facto ultimately was upheld, a number of key principles were explained by the court, including:

a Where an LPR seeks payment of a death benefit to themselves personally (i.e. not to the estate), they will be in a position of conflict, unless the will expressly permits the conduct;

b Where there is no express provision waiving conflict, an LPR should renounce their position before taking any active steps to seek personal payment of the death benefit;

c Alternatively, the LPR can seek the consent of all other LPRs (if any);

d In seeking the consent of the other LPRs, there is no obligation to also receive consent from each beneficiary under the will;

e Complications will likely arise where there is a sole LPR. In that instance, if they choose not to renounce their role, there would be an obligation to receive the informed consent of each potential beneficiary.

Ultimately, the decision is yet another reminder of the importance of a holistic approach to every estate plan involving superannuation entitlements.

Munro & Anor v Munro & Anor [2015] QSC 61

This case is particularly important because it highlights the potential consequences that can arise when a BDBN does not comply precisely with the requirements set out in the trust deed.

The case involved the deceased (Mr Munro) and his second wife who had established an SMSF. Mr Munro subsequently signed a BDBN form nominating the 'Trustee of Deceased Estate' as the death benefit recipient.

After the death of Mr Munro, the remaining trustee (his second wife) and her daughter (who was appointed as a co-trustee after Mr Munro's death) paid the death benefit to his second wife on the basis the BDBN was invalid.

Mr Munro's daughters from his first wife, who were the executors of his estate, applied for a declaration that the nomination form signed by Mr Munro was a valid BDBN and that the funds should be paid to his estate instead of his second wife.

The Court rejected the application and held the BDBN was not valid as it did not comply with the specific requirements of the SMSF's trust deed.

In particular, the trust deed only allowed nominations in favour of a dependant, or a LPR.

The Court held that even though Mr Munro may have intended for the LPR to receive his benefits, nominations had to be construed on their plain meaning.

Critically, the Court confirmed that the relevant definition of LPR under the Law is 'the executor of the will of a deceased person'. While the terms 'executor' and 'trustee' are often used interchangeably, the roles are legally distinct.

The Court also noted that SMSF BDBNs do not have to comply with the requirements in the Law (unless required by the SMSF's trust deed).

Stock (as Executor of the Will of Mandie, Deceased) v N.M. Superannuation Proprietary Limited [2015] FCA 612

This decision is another reminder of the fact that superannuation death benefits are not an estate asset.

Broadly the background was as follows –

a The member died without making any binding nomination for his superannuation benefits, although binding nominations were permissible;
b The member had made a non-binding nomination to his wife, however she predeceased him;
c The trust deed for the fund provided that if there was no binding nomination the trustee retained the discretion to pay a death benefit to the member's dependants or LPR;
d The trustee of the super fund resolved to pay the death benefit to the member's dependants, namely 3 adult children, in equal shares;

e The LPR challenged the distribution on the basis of comments in the member's will, including the fact that two of the adult children had entered into a settlement agreement with their father 20 years earlier confirming they would have no entitlement under his estate;

f Under the member's will, his estate made provision for grandchildren and the child who was not a party to the settlement the other two children had entered into.

In rejecting the LPR's challenge it was confirmed that superannuation is not an asset of an estate and a trustee is not bound to follow the directions of a will.

In particular, even if superannuation is specifically mentioned in a will, this does not make it an asset subject to the terms of the will. While a trustee may review a deceased member's will, it is not the role of a super fund trustee to attempt to resolve issues relating to their estate.

Rather, a trustee must independently determine the distribution of a death benefit, unless there is a valid binding death benefit nomination.

It was also confirmed that in making a determination, a super fund trustee need only show that their decision is fair and reasonable. Any court review of a trustee decision therefore did not need to analyse the trustee's processes or reasoning.

Index

Interested to learn more?

View has invested heavily to help advisers help their clients.

Some popular examples of adviser tools are as follows:

1. Subscribe to the free weekly blog posts:

http://blog.viewlegal.com.au/?m=1

To subscribe to the blog, simply enter your email address in the subscription box in the right hand column or alternatively, subscribe through your preferred RSS feed from your browser.

2. View Intellectual Property platform (VIP)

The VIP subscription platform provides you with free access to our webinars, as well as discounted access to our books, entity establishment, superannuation and estate planning solutions.

Even if you trial the VIP platform to update your own estate planning and structuring arrangements it represents fantastic value.

Learn more at—

http://viewlegal.com.au/view-vip-subscription-platform-2/

3. Education programs

View Legal specialises in all forms of adviser education and collaborative learning.

We are fortunate to regularly present to accountants, financial planners, other lawyers and risk advisers.

Our programs are tailored to meet your specific requirements and can be delivered in lengths ranging from 20 minute web-based updates to 5 day in-house courses (and every permutation in between) and formats including in person, webinar and video streaming. Our most popular sessions tend to be 90 minute team trainings, which can be recorded for future use.

A sample of some of our current topics is set out at the following link—

http://viewlegal.com.au/product-category/events/

Or simply stream or purchase DVD copies of previous programs via the following link—

http://viewlegal.com.au/recorded-webinars/

A Selection of Other Books from View Legal

For all the latest books please visit https://viewlegal.com.au/product-category/books/

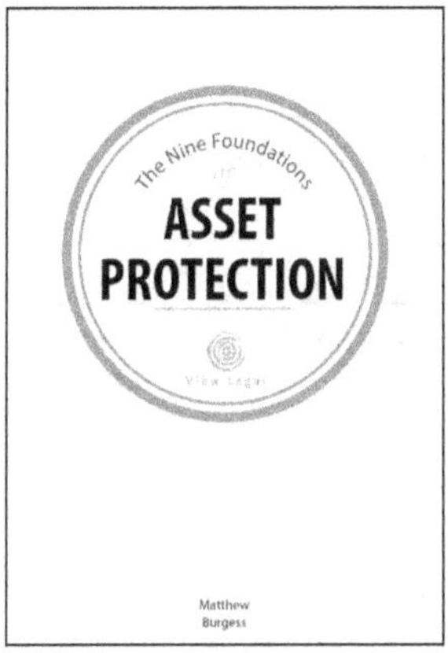

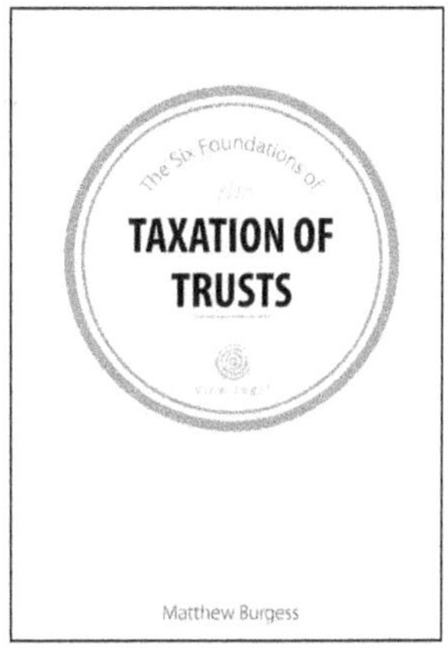

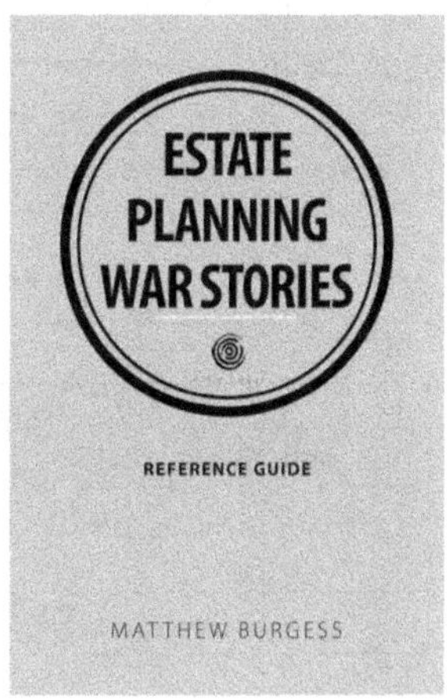

About View

At View Legal our mantra is to be 'for friends'.

In other words creating solutions and value propositions that are compelling to our friends.

To achieve our vision, we have set out to fundamentally and radically revolutionise access to high quality legal advice, in our areas of deep specialisation—structuring, tax, trusts, asset protection, business sales, estate and succession planning.

To help explain the approach View is taking to uniquely deliver valuable legal solutions, the following table lists 10 traditional ways law firms have operated (and, almost exclusively, continue to operate) and the new vision that View is built around.

Old view	View Legal
Bill clients on hourly rates (or various, increasingly elaborate, permutations on the theme) and have no particular interest in client perception of value	Customers provided up front 'SPS Guarantee'—that is service and price satisfaction is guaranteed with all work undertaken following upfront fixed pricing
Everything tracked on a timesheet. The longer something takes, the better	No timesheets. Sophisticated project management tools used to help ensure customer expectations are exceeded
Quality is defined by the law firm	Quality is defined by the customer
'Impressive' CBD office space, with 'dominant' fit outs	View meets where best suits customers. No permanent CBD space retained
Intellectual property is how we make money and should be guarded jealously	Intellectual property is how we create trust and should be shared freely
Lawyers striving to deliver near-perfect technical excellence	All service designed to be fit-for-purpose, aligning with collaboratively agreed customer objectives
Lawyers cultural focus on 'is this billable' for the firm	Lawyers cultural focus on 'is this valuable' for the customer
'Leveraging' of full-time lawyers to do the bulk of the work serving clients	Flexible work practices that match supply with demand
Constant focus on the 'need for diversity' of gender	Only focus on diversity of thought
Revenue growth the #1 goal	Exceeding customer expectations #1 goal

Significant inspiration provided by VeraSage. Partly adapted with permission of George Beaton, Beaton Capital.

If you would like to learn more about any of the above solutions or View more generally contact 1300 View 00 (1300 843 900), email mail@viewlegal.com.au or contact one of the founders listed at the foot of our home page at - http://viewlegal.com.au/

Testimonials

A selection of testimonials for presentations by View (including for organisations such as The Tax Institute, various law societies, Television Education Network, AMP, NAB and ALPMA) are as follows:

> Excellent session. Full of interactivity and practical examples/cases.
>
> I wanted to send you a quick note to say that I thought the session you presented was superb and certainly in my top 2 for the entire event.
>
> Your session was the one that we were able to take away the most useful information. We managed to totally can our latest project and built a new one by the time we hit the airport to head home!
>
> Thank you for your excellent presentation at the conference today. In a sentence, it was very inspiring.
>
> Your session was unreal. Very engaging, honest and fun.
>
> Your presentation was simply fantastic! A lesson in how to take the dull and boring and make it fun and entertaining.

www.ingramcontent.com/pod-product-compliance
Lightning Source LLC
LaVergne TN
LVHW022230200926
848481LV00006B/2203